CW00694140

NOCTON

THE LAST YEARS OF AN ESTATE VILLAGE

Collected by
Sheila Redshaw
and
Compiled by
Sue Morris

Sheila P. Redshaw
Sue Morris
18/10/2007

First Published in Great Britain in 2007 by Tucann Books
Text © Sue Morris & Sheila Redshaw
All rights reserved
Design © TUCANN*design&print*

No part of this publication may be reproduced or transmitted in any way or by any means, including electronic storage and retrieval, without prior permission of the publisher.

ISBN 9781873257807

Produced by: TUCANN*design&print*
19 High Street, Heighington, Lincoln LN4 1RG
Tel & Fax: 01522 790009
www.tucann.co.uk

CONTENTS

INTRODUCTION

Sheila Redshaw
Wellhead Lane
Nocton
April 2007

Dear Reader,

For some time, I have been wanting to write about life in Nocton, for future generations to read about.

I realised a long time ago that there is no plaque in Nocton to the men who died from this parish in the Second World War, nor any record of those men and women from our parish who served in the Armed Forces, so I have written to the War Graves Commission to find out who and where they died. I would like to acknowledge their sacrifice here within this book

I hope my story will convey to you what life was like in Nocton many years ago. With the help of Old Church Magazines, Newspaper Cuttings, Smiths Crisps magazines and photos, some taken in the early 1900's and shown to the village people on the Magic Lantern, will help me to illustrate what life was like.

In 1955, I married Fred Redshaw in All Saints Church, Nocton, fifty two years later I still live in Nocton. As you would expect many changes have taken place during that time. When I came to Nocton it was known as Smiths Potato Estates Ltd. It has changed hands several times since then, large insurance companies being the landlords and now belongs to a private owner, Mr Paul Clarke and is called Nocton Ltd and Nocton is no longer an Estate Village. My book is about some of the people of Nocton past and present, the working and living conditions, and social events. I dedicate this book to them, especially those who gave me so much information with such enthusiasm and energy. Last but not least, my sincere and grateful thanks to Sue Morris, (My Compiler) for her valuable help, advice and patience. Without her skills it would be impossible to forward this book for publication.

THE COMPILER'S NOTES

I have tried to develop each area from the time of the Ripons and then the Hodgsons, at the turn of the previous century, by using the 1891 and the 1901 Census records and then concluding at the turn of the last century. In reality, the last 120 years. The most important change that has occurred in that time, is the workforce. Even up to the 1950's there were 300 people employed on the Estate, and most of those were housed in Nocton or Dunston by the Estate. Now there are but a handful of employees living in tied cottages, all the rest of the dwellings along with their gardens have been sold off to people who do not work in the village. The Hall was "The Centre" of the Estate and Village activities in the 1890's, so I have started here and proceeded around the parish in an anticlockwise direction. So much material has been accumulated that the book would have been large and cumbersome, so

it was decided to write it in two volumes. The second volume will be centred around the work of Mrs Ireson, and the centre of the village – the school, church and the vicarage, and then back to the Hall during the time that RAF Nocton Hall Hospital was in residence.

While I have been working on this project, I have met so many interesting people, seen so many photographs – some personal, some of great historic interest, especially Chris Howard's Sugar Beet Photo Albums, and I have been off on wild goose chases about the late 8th century Triple Pin Set found at Fiskerton in 1826 which were given to the British Museum in 1858 and I believe was never in the hands of the Hodgsons as reported in a local newspaper in 1931.

I hope that you enjoy reading the book, or just looking at the photos.

Max Howard with his Prize Bull – "Nocton Rise Mercury" 1st in Class 1V and Champion of the Show, Lincoln Red Shorthorn Bull Show and Sale in April 1954 on the Carholme, Lincoln. This was his last day as President of the Society.

Shearling Ram "Nocton Rise Oracle". Champion Single Ram and winner of the 'Mrs Robert Wright Perpetual Challenge Cup' bred by Mr E M Howard. Lincoln Longwool Sheepbreeders Association First Sale at Cattle Market, Lincoln in 1948.

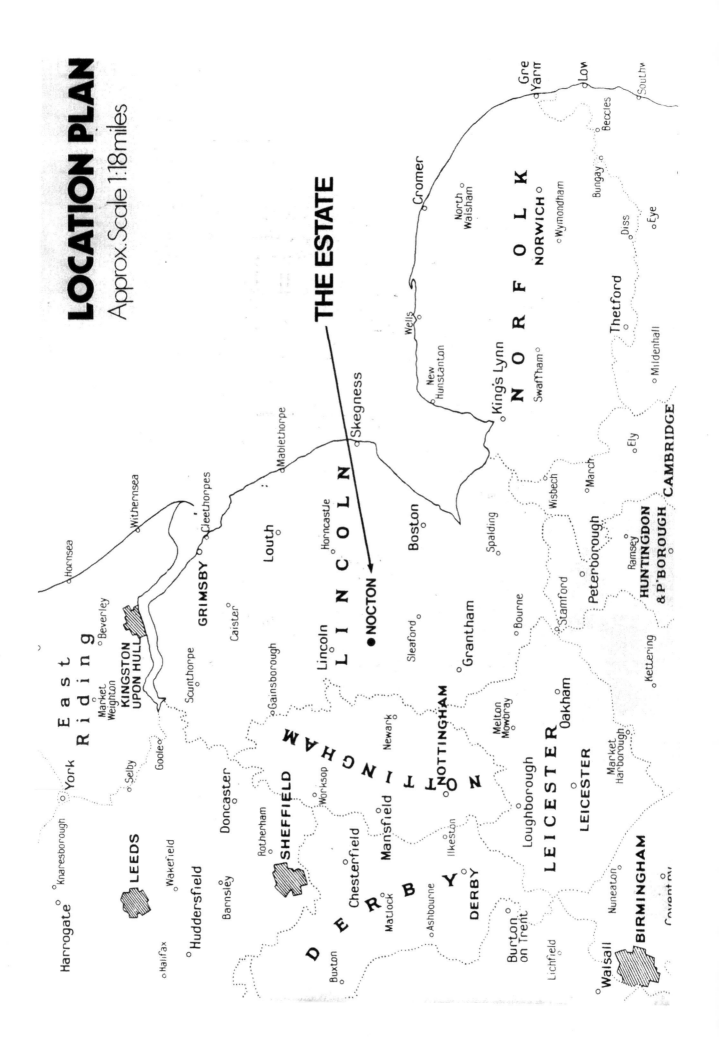

LOCATION PLAN
Approx. Scale 1:18 miles

THE ESTATE

NORFOLK

NORWICH

LINCOLN

● NOCTON

GRIMSBY

East Riding

KINGSTON UPON HULL

LEEDS

SHEFFIELD

NOTTINGHAM

DERBY

LEICESTER

BIRMINGHAM

HUNTINGDON & P'BOROUGH

CAMBRIDGE

Cromer
North Walsham
Wymondham
Bungay
Diss
Eye
Beccles
Gre Yarm
Low
South

Wells
New Hunstanton
King's Lynn
Swaffham
Ely
March
Wisbech
Thetford
Mildenhall

Skegness
Boston
Spalding
Bourne
Stamford
Peterborough
Ramsey

Horncastle
Sleaford
Grantham
Kettering

Mablethorpe
Louth
Lincoln

Withernsea
Cleethorpes
Caister
Gainsborough
Scunthorpe

Hornsea
Beverley
Market Weighton
Selby
Goole
Doncaster
Worksop
Newark
Melton Mowbray
Oakham

York
Harrogate
Knaresborough
Wakefield
Barnsley
Rotherham
Chesterfield
Mansfield
Ilkeston
Loughborough
Market Harborough

Huddersfield
Halifax
Matlock
Ashbourne
Buxton
Burton on Trent
Lichfield
Nuneaton
Leicester

Walsall
Covent ov

1824 Ordnance Survey Map of Nocton

DASHWOOD'S LIGHTHOUSE, LINCOLN HEATH, IN THE LAST CENTURY.

Dashwood's Lighthouse
Picture of Dunston Pillar lit on a stormy night, showing the four corner buildings.

CHAPTER ONE
Nocton – an Estate Village

Nocton – an Estate Village. What does this mean? The definition of an Estate village is "A Village wholly or largely built by a single gentry or aristocratic landowner in a place where he had his principle residence. Generally the housing would be architect designed and of a superior quality and the village might have a school and/or village hall to match." Another term often used is "A Closed Village" and sometimes a Town is also "A Closed Town" such as Spilsby where the Willoughby d'Eresby family from Grimsthorpe near Bourne, owned the local estate and all the land within the town.

Nocton falls within these parameters. There was a Manor house in Nocton in 1541 when King Henry VIII and Katherine Howard stayed with the young squire Thomas Wymbishe, a descendant of Norman d'Arcy. Nocton passed by marriage to the Townleys of Burnley in the latter part of the sixteenth century, and about 100 years later was bought by the Ellys family, in the 1670's. Charles Townley had been killed at Marston Moor with Royalist forces, whereas the purchaser of the estate had been a loyal servant of the Parliametary forces. Sir William Ellys built the magnificent seat of Nocton Hall in about 1690, old engravings show that it was an 'E' plan building with five turrets topped with cupolas.

Nocton Hall – An early print of Sir William Ellys's home (From a glass slide)

When his son died, his widow married Sir Francis Dashwood, who became Chancellor of the Exchequer in 1762, and did much to improve the land at Nocton, not only in promoting the Witham Drainage Bill in Parliament but in safeguarding the lives of travellers on the "dreary waste" of the heathlands by building Dunston Pillar.

NOCTON.

On the sides of the Pillar appear the following inscriptions:

North side.	*East side.*
TO LINCOLN, V. MILES.	DUNSTAN PILLAR.
South side.	*West side.*
FROM THE CITY CXX. MILES.	COLUMNAM HANC. UTILITATI PUBLICÆ. D. D. D. F. DASHWOOD. M. DCC. LI.

Dunston Pillar with the lantern on the top

In 1767, we find the Hobart family at the Hall entertaining on a lavish scale with a masquerade ball, the fame of which London hears. The Honourable George Hobart had a great influence on Nocton, for land improvement was given priority importance in the latter half of the eighteenth century. Representing himself as 'patron of the vicarage of the parish church' he destroyed the old church, as it was too near the hall, and rebuilt a small modest church in the present churchyard. He obtained a private Act of Parliament for the enclosure of the open lands and the commutation of the vicar's tithes. After the Heath was enclosed the lantern on Dunston Pillar was no longer needed, so a bust of George the Third was made in Coade Stone and this replaced the lantern, (the bust was taken off and the pillar reduced in height during the Second World War). George became third Earl of Buckingham, and his Countess, Albinia, was described as a notorious gambler and devotee of faro. When she won, there were lavish parties; when she lost, Nocton was mortgaged. He was followed by his eldest son,

Dunston Pillar with King George on the top

Nocton Hall built in 1842

View from Nocton Hall

Robert, in 1804, but he died in 1816 without a male heir so his title went to a nephew but the Nocton estate passed to his daughter, Lady Sarah Albina Hobart who had recently married Frederick John Robinson. Robinson was a great politician holding many senior posts in Government, including Prime Minister for less than a year, it was at this time that their son, George, was born. After his resignation from office, the Viscount was made the first Earl of Ripon in 1833, the same year that they set about improving the village life of Nocton by building the Almshouses. But in 1834 there was a terrible fire at the Hall, despite the use of a brand new fire engine; the building was burnt to the ground. Building work on the New Hall started after eight years, the architect being William Shearburn of Dorking, a Nocton born boy. His father Joseph Shearburn, the estate joiner oversaw the building work, which took ten years to complete at the cost of between £40,000 and £50,000. While this was going on, the Old Row was built in 1841, and the plans were being made for a new Church which was started in 1860, a year after the Earl died. Lady Sarah continued with the building of the church and had it dedicated to "All Saints", for the Earl's birthday was on November 1st. It was not quite complete when she died in April 1867, but her son, George, added the South aisle and the South Porch in 1872 "as a tribute of reverential

affection of his mother". George had the School built in 1869, the Ripon Row in 1850s and the Ten Row in 1878. These properties were built in the distinctive 'Gothic Revival' style. The Top and Bottom Lodges were also built to the same design, and the Pillars at Top Lodge were mounted by Griffins holding a Shield with the Ripon Coat of Arms.

Bottom Lodge coming from the Hall

Entering the Hall grounds from the Village

Entering the grounds from the Carriageway and the Railway Station– Top Lodge

Entering the grounds from the Bottom Lodge

large estate like Nocton and they must have talked about the coming of the railway. For the 1st of August 1882 was a day to remember as it was the opening of Nocton and Dunston Railway Station, on the Lincoln to Sleaford line, thus connecting Nocton to the outside world. So it was in 1889, that Lord Ripon sold Nocton Estate to George Hodgson, a self made man, born in 1819, who had been apprenticed to a mechanic. He then started work as a loom maker and by 1855, he had developed the Hodgson Power Loom which was famous not only in Bradford but worldwide. By 1889, he had received many highly regarded international trade honours for his loom and made a great deal of money.

He came to Nocton at the age of 70, but was unable to participate in all the sporting fun of the 7,300 acres estate, and he allowed his eldest son, John, to take over the running of the estate as a resident landlord. When John inherited Nocton estate in 1895, he, with his wife, Ann, set about creating an extensive lake north of the Lime Avenue which was fed with water from the beck in Dunston.

Lantern Slide of Annie daughter of Mr and Mrs John Hodgson and Mrs Chard, the Vicar's wife.

Lantern Slide of the Gardens

All this building work was going on while George was entering politics. At the age of 26, he had won a by-election for the Liberals in Huddersfield, which started a long and able political career including time at the Indian Office and the War Office. In January 1859, his father died and he inherited the title of Earl of Ripon and the Nocton estate and in the November he inherited from his uncle the title of Earl de Grey of Wrest and land at Studley Royal and Fountains Abbey as well as estates in Bedfordshire. In 1873, he surprised everyone by resigning as Lord Lieutenant of North Riding also his cabinet position and was received into the Roman Catholic Church. It was about this time that he met and formed a close friendship with George Hodgson, a banker and an industrialist from the West Riding of Yorkshire. They had much in common both being Liberal thinkers, politicians in their own right and believers in free trade. George Hodgson had bought an estate in the South of France and it was there that the Marquis of Ripon and his son Oliver spent many winter breaks, discussing and confiding about the financial strain of looking after a

An extract from the Church Magazine in 1900, states that " On Saturday evenings, the 26th of May, the 30th June, and the 28th of July, Mr and Mrs Hodgson invited the villagers to dance on the lawn to the west of the Hall; the Nocton and Dunston Band was in attendance and the Bandsmen were kindly entertained to supper afterwards". But John did not live very long to enjoy the country surroundings for he died in 1902, leaving his 25 year old son Norman to return from the Army. Norman had been fighting the Boers in South Africa and been promoted to Captain the previous year. He

View through the arch to the Church

Norman Hodgson drove a 1907 Rover 12 hp two seater open tourer car, similar to this picture

came to Nocton and gave the whole place a face lift. The Hall was redecorated and the hall grounds and gardens were restocked with shrubs and herbaceous plants, in an attempt to create one of the most beautiful gardens in England.

The greatest change to rural life, Nocton being no exception, was the coming of the motor car in the 1907. Up to this time, horses were the means of transport. John Hodgson believed he had the best turned out Hooper coach and four in the county. There were stables, coach house and a blacksmiths situated close to the Hall. At this time, the estate was farmed by Tenant Farmers, 26 in all with each farming about 300 acres. Some having their homesteads and farm buildings within the village curtilage, while others lived and worked on the Heath or down on the Fens. Norman had a new set of farm buildings erected at Park Farm in 1913, now known as Wrays yard. But changes were ahead. World War 1 had broken out and Tenant

farmers and their work force set about increasing food production, and potatoes was the crop that was increased the most. Also required was the supply of manpower for the front, so gradually experienced and valuable men and women left Nocton, some never to return. There is a memorial, in the church, to all those that went to fight in the World War I. In 1917, Norman decided that the Hall should become a convalescent home for the American Officers wounded on the front, and so the Hodgson family moved to Embsay House where they remained until the estate was sold in 1919. The Rev Chard wrote in the Parish Magazine "There has been widespread regret at the departure of Mr N.Hodgson and family which took place on July 26th 1919. Though anticipated for some time, it was only to be expected that after so many years in our midst many regrets would be expressed, especially by the older members of the community who had known them so long. We can only express the good wishes of all for every blessing to follow them to their new home and work, and assure them our constant interest in their concerns, and also a hearty welcome when ever they can come amongst us."

And so it came to pass that Norman and Ida did return to Nocton, for they are both buried in the Churchyard. Norman was born on Christmas Eve 1873 and lived for seventy three years all but one day for he died on 23.12.1946. Ida, his wife was born September 6th 1889 and died on 13th June 1967.

Eustace Pask mowing the lawns

CHAPTER 2
Major changes were to take place in the coming years.

The Estate was bought by Messrs W.H.Dennis and Sons from Kirton in 1919.

William and Sarah Dennis

The legendary William Dennis, a farm foreman's son, who in 1861, left Horsington, near Horncastle, at the age of 20, and set off to walk the twenty miles to Kirton, carrying his scythe, his sickle, and his gathering rake. On arrival he sat down on a milestone outside of the church and tossed a coin, should he stay in Kirton or should he move on? It was heads for Kirton, tails for moving on. It landed head up. He was taken on by a local Farmer that very afternoon, and William soon realised that the rich silt of the area was ideal for growing potatoes. He was hard working and thrifty. In 1871, he made his first land purchase of six acres on which he built a house and started farming on his own. His potato enterprise continued to grow and he went into partnership with his five sons. He bought more and more land during the years of the depression and at one time they were farming 20,000 acres mostly in Lincolnshire, with some in Huntingdonshire and Cambridgeshire. By 1914, he and his sons had made their fortune.

John when he was Mayor of Westminster

All his sons were involved in the Business. John, the eldest, was in charge in London and New York, and became Mayor of Westminster as well as being the MP for a Birmingham constituency. He worked for the Ministry of Food in Whitehall as their Potato Controller during the First World War, his third wife was Evangaline Brewster from New York, who died in 1919 and was buried in Nocton Churchyard. Their second son, Joseph, assisted John in London, Jersey, St Malo and elsewhere in Europe. He was a keen sportsman and racing man.

Third son, Herbert, worked for the business in South Lincolnshire, managing Nocton Hall Estate from 1919 and buying it in 1925. He was a dedicated countryman, a keen shooting and hunting man. Thomas, the fourth son, was a brilliant linguist and spent much time travelling in the service of the potato, and was for many years Chairman of the Lincolnshire Standard paper. The youngest son, Frank, bought Frampton Hall near Kirton where they had all grown

Herbert "Taffy" Dennis

up. He assisted in the running of the great enterprise especially during the First World War when more and more acres of potatoes were required for the Nation.

Back to Nocton. It all happened in 1919. William Dennis bought Nocton Hall Estate. William and Sarah's third son Herbert came to live in the Hall at Nocton, along with his wife, Ethel and some of the family of nine children.

Ethel with one of their daughters

On the 6th August in Kirton Church, Herbert's daughter Annie, of Frampton Hall, Kirton married Major Leonard Webber, of Nocton, who was to be the land agent for the Nocton Hall Estate and they came to live in Embsay House.

The wedding of Annie Dennis and Leonard Webber, 9th August 1919

The beautiful long silk train that Annie wore on her wedding day had come from New York, and one can only presume that it was Evangeline, her sister-in-law, who had been responsible for the shipping of such finery. But sadly it was on 9th September that

Annie and Major Webber in their car outside of Embsay House

Evangeline Brewster Dennis died and was buried in Nocton Churchyard, she had slipped on a banana skin and broken her hip. One happy occasion and then five weeks later a very sad group of people gathered here in Nocton.

It was between 1919 and 1925 that the tenant farmers were given notice and gradually they gave up their holdings to the new owners who wanted to "Take the land in hand" that is, to farm the estate as a whole. This left many houses and farmsteads on the Heath and down the Fen empty. But not every one gave in, as the Particulars of Sale dated 1925 lists the "Schedule of the Estate as Occupied" that two Tenant Farmers (Howards at Nocton Rise and Wrays at Park Farm) were still farming nearly 700 acres between them. For William had died in 1924 and his empire was to be sold. The Nocton Estate was auctioned on 28th day of July 1925 at the Estate Room, 20, Hanover Square, London W.1, at 2.30 o'clock. His son Herbert purchased the Estate, which included 6,986a 2r 10p., the Stone built Elizabethan Style Mansion with a Billiard Hall, Ball Room and many other rooms too numerous to mention!. The gardens were described as "The Pleasure Grounds" with sweeping lawns, woodland walk, ancient fish pond, walled kitchen garden, and an Orchard. Also included were several properties, a Gardener's House, Coachman's Cottage and a Farmery.

Mr Herbert Dennis bought Nocton Hall Estate and continued to live at the Hall until he moved to the Manor House in 1927. His granddaughter, Yvonne, was 7 years old when he moved, and she recalled that her grandfather was a very strict person, and that she used to go between Embsay House and the Manor House. So it was at this time that the Hall with its grounds and the farming side of the Estate separated. But it was a year earlier, in 1926, that Major Webber bought a large quantity of ex W.D. track and rolling

Major Webber doing his rounds as Land Agent for the Estate.

stock from an army dump in Arras in France which had been destined for the 1916 Somme offensive but arrived too late to be put into service.

Tractor with a five foot wheel pulling a plough, (photo believed to have been taken in France), with Major Webber in the drivers seat.

The same tractor.

A small section of one and a half miles had been laid earlier at Wasp's Nest and the wagons had been pulled by horses. The advantages of such a railway on the rich but poorly drained fen land were obvious. So the 35 miles of track were laid out all around the estate in such a way that every field had a link to the "Railhead". Clay was dug from a pit in the Big Wood and used to form a base to prevent the rails from sinking into the peat fens. Six engines and 90 wagons were involved in carrying 17,000 tons of produce each year. Chitted potatoes were sent down to the fen for planting and the resulting harvest was transported to the Railhead, which was linked to a siding on the Main Line at Nocton and Dunston Station, where the crop would have been sorted and graded and then sent off to markets all over the country. The track was laid down the fen to the Witham Bank, where a gantry with a mechanical grab lifted the sugar beet across the river to the Bardney Sugar Beet Factory which had opened in 1924. This allowed all the sugar beet to be transported directly to the Bardney Factory thus avoiding the use of horses and carts and later lorries using the roads. As the estate employed about 300 people, the railway was put to every conceivable use, including delivering tanks of drinking water to the isolated cottages and crew yards in the fen. There are references to collecting the congregation for church, and operating a postal service with the guards van carrying letter boxes. The railway crossed the bridle path to Dunston and the main Lincoln to Sleaford Road.

The Estate Railway crossing the Bridle Path

It also crossed the main Lincoln to Sleaford Road.

Mr Herbert Dennis was a keen sportsman and on Shoot Days, there was a special train that waited at the Nocton Station for the "Guns" to arrive and they would embark onto the 20 foot long coach which had glass windows that wound up and down and was panelled in oak. There were ten swivel seats and legend has it that it was originally fitted out for the "Brass Hats" to tour the Western Front, and was known with affection as the "Queen Mary" after the Royal train. The coach was followed by the wagons for the beaters and loaders, one of which was still inscribed "Cinque Chevaux ou Vingt Hommes".

(Below) One of the many uses for the railway. Taffy can be seen in the centre with his characteristic hat, while Major Webber is standing in the front row on the extreme right.

Frank and "Taffy" Dennis with his dog "Don"

Conventional Tractors were also used on the Estate.

Mr Dennis and Major Webber inspecting a new tractor.

During the time that Herbert and his wife, Ethel, lived at Nocton Hall, it was the custom to entertain the local hunt on the front lawn at least once a year.

The Blankney Foxhounds Meet outside of Nocton Hall

This next photo was taken outside of Embsay House mid 1920's, showing the men dressed as if to go hunting. Was "The Meet" at Embsay House that year? Left to right Unknown person, Derek Young, unknown lady, Annie Webber, Yvonne Webber holding her doll and Major Leonard Webber.

Outside of Embsay House dressed for hunting mid 1920's

"The Meet" was at the Cross in Metheringham outside of the Star and Garter.

Blankney Hunt Meet at Metheringham in the mid 1920's

This was also taken in the early 1920's, because the Statue in the Remembrance Garden is so very white and the shrubs around the wall are still very young. Nell Turner, as a little girl of four, carried the key, on a velvet cushion, to open the gates on the dedication day. Her father had been killed in the War and the statue was designed from a photo of her father.

The Dennises and the Webbers liked their Cars, and here are four photos.

Taken outside of Embsay House

A closer look at the cars

Annie is sitting in the passenger's seat while Yvonne is arranging the picnic hamper

The Chauffeur is waiting outside of the Manor House sometime after 1927

Herbert died on 31st August 1938 and his ashes were scattered at Abbey Hill on a very wet and rainy day. This is an account of the day.

"A colleague, who attended the funeral service at Nocton of Mr J.H.Dennis, told me that the ceremony was the strangest in which he had ever taken part. The body had been cremated and at the express wish of Mr Dennis the ashes were scattered over the earth. The last part of the journey from the church to the burial ground was across a barren uneven field in an isolated part of Nocton Fen, where once the ruins of an Abbey stood. The burial ground itself was surrounded by a wooden fence which was hung with wreathes, among them was a wreath of wheat ears and cornflowers. Four young poplar trees had been planted in this enclosure, in which Mr Dennis's two eldest sons scattered his ashes."

A message on one of the Wreathes read "Good Hunting Pop."

"Taffy" Dennis's last resting place on Abbey Hill

One of the wreaths

During the 1960's and 1970's the four poplar trees were a distinct feature on the skyline of Abbey Hill, however now there is no sign of them at all.

Mrs Ethel Dennis moved away from Nocton and we have two photos of her in her later life.

Ethel Dennis left Nocton and is pictured here with her dog

Another photo with her eldest son John.

The Estate was sold in 1938 to Frank Smith the founder of Smith's Potato Crisps.

When Herbert moved from the Hall to the Manor House about 1927 many people have thought that the Hall was left empty. But according to the 1937 Kelly's Directory, Nocton Hall had become a School with Mr C.J. Cruikshank as the Head Master, formerly from Emsworth House, Emsworth, Hampshire. According to the Prospectus, it was a Preparatory School for boys 6 to 14 years of age for the Public Schools and the Navy. Nocton Hall was lighted by electricity and centrally heated. All the dormitories were light and airy rooms and the classrooms were all large. The aim of the school was to provide a good Education in an atmosphere as nearly as possible like that of a Home, and the health and happiness of the boys was placed before every other consideration. The catering and welfare of the School was entirely under the personal supervision of the lady owner, who was in permanent residence, and great care was exercised over diet and only the best of everything was provided. Fruit and Vegetables were grown on the premises. An experienced Matron was in residence.

The Prospectus goes on to say that the School curriculum included

ENGLISH:

CLASSICS: Grammar, Latin, Composition
Greek (if desired), Literature
History

MODERN LANGUAGES:
Geography, French
General Knowledge

MATHEMATICS:

DIVINITY: Old and New Testament
Gymnastics and Physical Drill

The following extras:-
Drawing, Music, Boxing, Carpentry,
Riding, Dancing.

Physical Training Exercises were held for a short period each morning. Outdoor Games included Cricket, Tennis, Associated Football and Hockey. The organisation of the Games and the coaching of the 1st XI was under the personal supervision of Mr Cruikshank, who had played a great deal of First class amateur football and cricket.

Fees were payable in advance and a Term's notice (or a Term's Fees) were required before a boy could be withdrawn from Nocton Hall.

Boys over 10 years of age.........................45 Guineas
Boys under 10 years of age.......................40 Guineas

Optional charges are :-
Piano ....3 Guineas
Dancing..2 Guineas
Drawing...1 Guinea
Boxing...1 Guinea
Carpentry...1 Guinea
Riding..4 Guineas

Extras :- Laundry charges 1½ Guineas per Term. Stationery 5s. per Term

It goes on to say "A reduction in the School Fees is made for the sons of Army and Naval Officers and the sons of Clergy, and also in the case of brothers."

The School Outfitters were:- Messrs Swan and Edgar, Piccadilly Circus, London, W.1

The School Colours were Royal Blue and Black. The boys wear grey flannel suits and grey flannel shirts (with the addition of grey woollen sweater for the winter).

White shirts for games, and during the summer. Grey tweed suits are worn on Sundays by the smaller boys and black jacket and striped trousers by the elder boys.

Special arrangements were made to meet any of the boys at King's Cross (London) station by one of the masters, and escort them to Nocton Hall and return them in the same way at the end of Term. Also Holiday arrangements could be made for the boys to remain at Nocton Hall if their parents were abroad.

Ann Barney (a great grand daughter of Herbert Dennis) allowed a photo of some school boys to be scanned for this book, and now that the above prospectus has come to light, the little pieces of jig saw are fitting together. It is only recently that it has come to light that Alice Elliott was "the lady owner, who was in permanent residence". Also, the photos of staff at Nocton Hall with the date of 1937, begin to explain their presence.

Nocton Hall School Boys sitting at a Trestle table

Margaret Franklin

Nora Harrison, Margaret Franklin, Mr and Mrs Swift, and Dorothy Chambers.

CHAPTER 3
Moving away from the Hall

The Gardener's House was built by Lady Sarah Hobart for her gardener who came to Nocton from Yorkshire.

Gardeners House and Kitchen Garden - Early 1910's

From the 1891 Census – The entry for The Nocton Hall Gardens states that a John Ridsdale was the Gardener and he was born in Bilton, Yorkshire and Mary, his wife was born in West Wetton also in Yorkshire, they had three children, the eldest son, Fred, was born in Nocton, now aged 21, and he was a Railway Clerk. So the Gardener and his wife came to live in Nocton before 1870. During the time that the Hodgsons were living in the Hall, it is recorded that the Head Gardener was more interested in the perfection of the Chrysanthemum than creating the most beautiful garden in England. For having delegated the daily tasks to the Junior Gardeners, the Head Gardener was often to be found in one of the greenhouses with his Chrysanthemums working on a project. His reward was winning the most coveted prize for Chrysanthemums at the RHS Hall in Westminster, a prize that he won for three consecutive years, but not sure who collected the trophy Mr Hodgson or Mr Ridsdale. By the time of the 1901 Census, there was no mention of John Ridsdale or his family living in the village. James Montgomery was a Gardener and had been born in Scotland forty seven years earlier. He lived with his wife Violet who had been born in Finchley, London and they had a Boarder, P. Kent, who was an Estate Clerk.

In 1891, Thomas and Sarah Mills lived in the "Nocton Hall Stables" and he was described as a Coachman, both of them had been born in Colchester in 1851. There had been a change of Coachman by 1901, as Albert Goodwin from St John's Wood in London had taken up this post with his wife Jessie who had been born in Scotland.

By the early 1910's Charles Richardson was one of the Grooms.

Coachman's Lodge – Early 1910's

The Stables with Charles Richardson one of the Grooms with one of the Hunters and her Foal – Early 1910's

What happened next? One can only presume that the gardener and his assistants carried on looking after the gardens when it was a convalescent home for the wounded American soldiers, then for Mr Dennis and then during the time of Nocton Hall School. In 1948 the Estates Company sold the Hall and 200 acres to the Air Ministry and by 1951 it was a General Military Hospital.

The Gardener's House along with the Orchards and the two walled gardens including the greenhouses were included in this deal, as well as the Coach house, the Lodge and the Stables. In 1985, these properties were included in the Sale by order of The Secretary of State for Defence. Soon after this sale, the first three properties were sold to individuals who have all transformed them into lovely stone homes and the Stables was turned into a Nursing Home for the Elderly.

The Woodyard with Fred Redshaw filling up a tractor in the 1950's.

Gardeners House July 1985

Garden and the Garden House 1988

Also mentioned in the 1925 Sale Particulars was the Farmery, described as Stabling for three (horses), Smithy and Shoeing Shed, four-bay Wagon Shed, Crewyards, & Wood Shed. This set of buildings was used in the Smith's Potatoes times as the Woodyard.

It has been recalled that up to 100,000 thatching pegs a year were made and used for thatching the ricks of the Estate, these were made from hazel that was coppiced in the hedgerows and in the woods of the Estate. There

is a set of Coats of Arms built into the stonework of the buildings on the Southside, and there are some beautiful white glazed bricks in one of the rooms. During the time that the RAF were in residence these buildings were used to store rations and vehicles. There is planning permission to convert the buildings into two dwelling, but for the time being the place is boarded up, and is the home for rare bats.

Tidying up the Woodyard - July 2006

Inside the Barn is a blocked up doorway which would have lead to the Coachman's Lodge

Another room with the white glazed bricks.

Moving on, we pass on your left the new Persimmons development in what was the Fishponds for the old Hall, and latterly as a water supply in case of Fire. And on your right is "The Park", the married quarters of the RAF Nocton Hall that were sold in 1988 to Blue Boar Developers, who in turn sold all the properties to individuals. And all the spare pieces of green areas have been bought by Mr Sowerby who is in the process of building 87 new homes.

Onto Potterhanworth Road. Manor Court now stands in what was Manor Farmyard until the late 1980s.

Potterhanworth Road

For many years Mr and Mrs Robert Scoley occupied the Manor Farm, and when Robert Scoley died in 1875, Mrs Emma Scoley moved to the "Almshouse" where she lived until 1891 when she moved to her daughter's home in Newark here she died in September 1901. There is more information about the Scoley families of Nocton and Potterhanworth in the Appendix.

Information gleaned from the 1891 census, mentions that George Dalton aged 70 and a widower lived at Manor Farm with his 23 year old son and a daughter of the same age. Also living there was John Reynolds, 23, a Mason, who had been born in Blankney, and two Farm Servants, both aged 22. There was a 20 year old female Domestic Servant, Doris Mountcastle who had been born in Ingham. In those days the Daltons would have been tenant farmers, living in the Farmhouse and using the Farm buildings for their stock and farming the land around the farmstead. It was in the time of the Dennises that the farm buildings and land were "taken in hand" and an employee would have lived in the farmhouse. It was in the late 1990's that the Nocton Ltd sold the Farmhouse.

Manor Farmhouse in the 1980's

Manor Farmhouse in the 1900's.

Front Porch of Manor Farmhouse in the 1950's

Smiths Potato Estates kept their famous Herd of Shorthorn Cattle in this Farmyard as well as several Bulls in the 1960's.

Shorthorn Cattle in Manor Farmyard in the early 1960's

Cattle Crush early 1960's - l to r Dan Wilford, Walter Tomlinson, Derek Hubbard, and Jim Rasen.

Manor Farmyard in the 1970's

Manor Farmyard in the 1980's

One solitary building remaining in 1988.

One of the new houses in Manor Court in 1992.

The Farmyard was sold for building in the late 1980's and the first houses were completed in Manor Court in 1992.

The Tomlinson family lived in the Farmhouse until the late 1990's when they moved to Branston.

The Tomlinsons lived at the Manor Farmhouse for many years and here are five of their sons Scything corn.

Hall Lodge is on your left on one of the many right angled bends in the Village. It was one of the entrances used in the days of Lord Ripon and sold to the Air Ministry in 1948, and later sold on by the RAF in July 1985 and after many alterations and additions it now is a good sized family home.

Hall Lodge – July 1985

Hall Lodge in 1993

There was an old cottage opposite the Lodge called the Avenue, Ann and Brian Hewis moved there on their marriage in 1959 and their son, David was born there. There was an outside toilet, only cold running water in the kitchen, with a door to the steep flight of stairs to two adjoining bedrooms which had concrete floors, and the windows looked out over the beck and the road. Hot water was obtained from a boiler beside the range, and was ladled out, and the oven was on the other side of the range. There had been no improvements made in the seven years that the Hewises lived there and they moved to one of the new Council Houses in 1966. It was then condemned and demolished. Mr and Mrs Rodham bought the site and built a bungalow and turned the Garden into a blaze of colour with flowers, Daffodils, Tulips, Roses and

An old photo of the house in the Avenue

The Rose Garden – 1985

Tulips in the Rose garden in 1988

Gladioli, these they sold to the visitors who were visiting patients at RAF Nocton Hall Hospital. Mrs Rodham was the Brown Owl for the Nocton Hall Brownie Pack for many years. Mrs Ward, who had lived in this cottage many years ago, was one of the polio victims from the local outbreak in August 1950. Ripon Row was so named after Frederick Robinson, first Earl of Ripon, who gave the four cottages to be used as almshouses, during his lifetime (1783 -1859). His son, George, continued to support the cottages. A directory of 1856, states that there are four cottages for the free use of the poor, and we presume the needy. In the 1881 census a resident by the name of Emma

Scoley, widow, 69, was living in one of these cottages. (She had been living at the Manor Farmhouse until her husband died) By 1891, they were being used as estate workers cottages.

Ripon Row has looked much the same for many years, this was taken 1981.

Behind the Ripon Row there was the Village Bakehouse, one can only presume that there was a large oven in this building and that the bread was sold to the villagers.

The Old Bakehouse that was situated behind Ripon Row and was taken down in the late 1980's.

Blankney Huntsmen passing Ripon Row in 1988

There are several photos of the front and rear gardens of No 20 taken in 1988 before Mrs S Redshaw moved to the bungalow in Wellhead Lane. There is now a group of three new stone properties that have been recently built in the gardens of Ripon Row and part of the Manor Farmhouse garden.

CHAPTER 4
Wellhead Lane through the Ages

Cattle roaming near the Old Post Office, built in 1833

The Old Post Office is on the corner of Wellhead Lane and was built in 1833. There is a record, in a church magazine, of the marriage on 30th July 1919 of Miss S. Smith, whose mother Mrs Smith lived at the Post Office. Miss S. Smith married Mr A. J. Smith of Horncastle at Nocton Church with a large congregation present. They went to Skegness for their honeymoon and were to make their new home in Horncastle.

A little later the Pygotts lived there and on Albert's retirement in 1961 he was interviewed by a reporter from the Standard. Albert was born in 1888, and was a lad of 15 when he first started work at Nocton Hall, and it wasn't until he was 72 years old that he retired, after working continuously for 57 years on the same estate. He started work in the gardens of the Hall when Mr Hodgson drove a "four in hand", and the big stone house was run by a small army of servants. He recalled the selling of the hall and he was then transferred to the Woodyard and became a woodman – a position he held until he retired. He was made a charge hand of his department in 1930, his job entailed planting trees, cutting them down and maintaining the fences on the estate. He was presented with a gold watch to mark 21 years of working for the Smiths Potato Estates. He declared that his proudest possessions are his family. "We have six children, and we are proud of all of them" he said. Mr Pygott married a Nocton girl on April 16th 1913 at Nocton Parish Church, and they had three sons and three daughters and they all married. Their eldest daughter lived in Toronto, another lived in Nocton while the third lived in Potterhanworth. Two of their sons moved to Hertfordshire, one was a Police Inspector at Watford while the other was a manager for a large grocery firm, and their third son lived in Nocton. At the end of May 1955 Albert and his wife set off on journey of a lifetime to visit their daughter in Canada, whom they had not seen for fourteen years. They were walking up the gang plank of the liner in Liverpool, when the stewards walked off, but they refused to return to work, so the Pygotts had to come back to Nocton, then a message came to say that a Greek liner was available in Southampton, so the luggage was retrieved from Liverpool and they set off and saw the Niagara Falls, Quebec, Montreal and the National Park. The Pygotts were a couple who did not believe in moving house a deal, for they had lived 20 years in Hall Lodge and 21 at the Old Post Office before they moved to their present home, and Albert told the reporter that he wanted to live there for 21 years, but that was not to be for he died the following year.

Mr and Mrs Albert Pygotts

The Ten Row is then on your left. This terrace of houses should have been five sets of semi-detached houses, but the land agent left in charge, while the Earl of Ripon and his son were busy with other affairs, economised and built the terrace.

Wellhead Lane in the early 1900's showing a horse with a load of hay or corn, most likely coming up from one of the farms on the Fen and making its way to either Nocton Rise or to the Wright's farm up on the Heath.

Wellhead Lane showing a pony and cart

The employees of Smiths' Potatoes lived in these tied cottages and we are fortunate to have some photos and reminisces of life there in the 1950's. In 1953, Arthur and Elsie Horton, and their two young children, moved into no. 7 The Ten Row. They were the youngest couple in the Ten Row for all the other inhabitants were elderly, with the Carratts living at no. 2. John Gathercole had the first car shown outside his house in 1953. The road was made of cinders and if there was a pot-hole, it was soon filled up with the cinders from the fireplace.

John Gathercole's car parked outside his home in the mid 1950's.

Arthur drove a van for the estate and often parked it opposite the house when he came home for lunch. He was very proud the day he took delivery of a "New Van".

Arthur Horton

Brand new Smiths Potato Estates Ltd van.

Elsie was not impressed when she first saw the house on moving in day, and had Mr Ireson (the General Estate Manager) round to discuss the problems about the Bathroom and Toilet. There was a Toilet, it was behind the yard door in a little hut, but it was a bucket that needed emptying a least twice a week down in the garden across the road. There was no Bathroom, the tin bath was brought into the living room, usually on a Friday night, and the hot water was carried in buckets from the old wash copper in the yard. The washing up was done in a bowl on a table in the "Shed" and the laundry washing was done in the yard with a Dolly Peg. And all the cooking was done on a range in the living room. Each dwelling had a yard with a high stone wall with one external door, the Toilet was behind the door along with the coal, on the other side was the copper for heating water, diagonally opposite the outside door was the drain or "sink" and on the remaining wall was "The Shed", which not only served as a kitchen but as a store for the bikes overnight. The water was supplied by a Lion Water Pump, which served the ten houses for drinking and washing – can you imagine 10 housewives all wanting water at the same time on a Monday morning to fill their coppers.

And Marion on her cousin's motor bike

This area was the Playing field before it was made into gardens with washing lines and it has changed many times since, now being individual gardens. These three youngsters lived in The Row at this time.

Lion pump similar to the one used by the ten residents of the 10 Row in the mid 1950's

In the winter of 1963-4 alterations were made to the properties, and Elsie can remember Christmas 1963 well, for all the floor boards had been lifted leaving just two planks to walk to the range. An extension was added to the house with a bathroom, which had an inside toilet, bath and hand basin, and a kitchen, with an electric socket for a cooker, which she had to buy as the range had been taken out from the living room.

After the alterations in 1964 – Arthur and Roland playing darts in the yard

1962 – Before the alterations – Roland with his push bike

Marion riding Roland's Scooter through the builder's rubble.

Arthur worked for the Estate for 16 years. Elsie worked on the Wards at the RAF Nocton Hall, and she received the RAF AOC's Commendation in 1979 "for acting over and above her daily duties". The same year the family moved to a Council House on Lincoln Road, and later Arthur and Elsie moved into one of the Council's bungalows, where Elsie still lives.

A report from the Lincolnshire Chronicle dated Saturday December 29 1951.

Nocton Couple Celebrate Diamond Jubilee.
Mr and Mrs John Thomas Carratt, of No 2, Ten Row, Wellhead Lane, Nocton celebrate their 60th wedding anniversary on Monday. They were married at Nocton All Saints Church on December 24, 1891. When the reporter called to see them, they were staying with their daughter, Mrs S. E. Cross of 20 John Street Lincoln. Days of when farm workers used to go to Lincoln only once a year were recalled by Mr Carratt, who started work at the age of 10, said they never used to wear fine cloth suits in those days. "We used to reckon we were well dressed when we used to go to church wearing billycock hats, Fustian cord trousers and a silk handkerchief round the neck". (Fustian was a course cotton material with a pile like velvet). To this very day, Mr Carratt prefers the silk handkerchief for neck wear, and it is only on very rare occasions that he can be persuaded to forsake it for a tie.

Mr and Mrs J Carratt celebrating their Diamond Wedding Anniversary 24th December 1951

Both Mr and Mrs Carratt are aged 83, Mr Carratt was born at Helpringham Fen, while his wife was a native of Dunston, but has lived in Nocton since she was four. For sixteen years they were newsagents at Nocton and during the First World War worked at Potterhanworth factory manufacturing waterproof covers for Army use. Referring to the changes which have taken place since they were first married, Mr Carratt said "I don't think they have bettered anything."

He was a horseman all his younger part of his life, and comments "I cannot see as they have improved anything with doing away with horses. We used to get up at 3.30 to four o'clock in the mornings – there was no half day on Saturday, and we had very little rest on Sunday." Mrs Carrattt added that for many years they only earned 12s 6d a week but it seemed to go as far as the present day wages. They also told that some of the Ten Row tenants in the early 1900's were employed by the council breaking stone to repair the roads and one man even had a cart for stone removing. Both are still very active and their health is good. They have a Family of five sons and two daughters. Mrs Carratt is an enthusiastic member of the Nocton Women's Institute, and also the Village Hall Social Club. The Women's Institute have presented Mrs Carratt with a diamond wedding gift of a brooch and Mr Carratt with a bottle of brandy.

The bungalows in Wellhead Lane

The set of four semi-detached bungalows for the elderly were the brainchild of Mr Harry Jackson, who was a North Kesteven councillor in 1969, when he persuaded the "powers that be" to build them in Nocton and not add to the stock already in Metheringham, Ald G.W. Hutson spoke up for Nocton saying that Metheringham had had a fair crack of the whip, and "to keep such villages alive, you have to put incentive there, by erecting bungalows, you are keeping it in the family and the young married couples will no doubt settle down and keep the village alive". They have allowed the older villagers to give up a large house to the next generation and remain in the village where they have lived for a long time near their friends and relations. The next houses on the left were built by NK Council, over many years. On the right hand side was the old Sheep Wash, which would have required fast flowing water to wash the sheep before they were shorn in the early summer. This area was later allocated to the householders of the Ten Row for their gardens and toilets before the days of flushed loos!

Further up Wellhead Lane outside of the Telephone Exchange

The telephone exchange building is still standing and is now used as a garden shed by Al and Barbara Bee who live in the house that was built for the District Nurse in the 1950's.

Telephone Exchange now used as a garden store

The District Nurse lived in this house until it was sold in 1990s

In this next group of houses, several families lived since the houses were built, they have had and still have an influence on Village Life. Jean was born in a cottage at Wasps Nest and grew up in one the Game keepers' Cottages, and she married Frank Meechan in September 1952.

Jean Stiff and Frank Meechan's Wedding - September 1952

Frank was the postman for 34 years until his death in 1992, and in his spare time he bred new varieties of Clematis, "Frankie" being one. Jean was a secretary at RAF Nocton Hall Hospital for many years, until it was closed down. Jean is a member of the WI and has been Secretary for at least ten years. She was an active member of the Friendship Club, until it folded.

Eileen and George Moulds live in this area and this piece is about their life in Nocton.

It was July 1952, Eileen was working in an office in Bootle when she decided to take a "Working Holiday on the Land" and she came to Metheringham Airfield. Quite a journey by train from Liverpool. On the first night a group of girls walked to the pub in Martin, and there was George selling Raffle Tickets for the Martin Football Club. They went across to the Dance in the Village Hall opposite the pub and the two started talking, they went out several times during that fortnight. Eileen has often said "I didn't win a prize but I ended up with a husband". They kept in touch through letters and visits – most people did not have a phone in their homes at that time. The couple were married at St. Robert Bellarmines Church, Orrell on Thursday 25th of March 1954, 'The Feast of the Annunciation' the only day in Lent when flowers and hymns were allowed. George had been allocated a tied cottage in the Old Row as he was to work for the

Eileen and George Moulds' Wedding 25th March 1954

Smiths Crisps Estate from Lady Day, at £6 per week. The rent for the cottage was four shillings a week. Life in a rural village was some what different to living and working in a city. The cottage had one electric light and no power points everything was cooked on the fire and all the water had to be collected from the pump outside. There was an outside toilet - none of the modern conveniences that she had left behind in Bootle.

Eileen enjoyed village life but found it was not easy living off George's wages, so in the summer applied at Lincoln for an office post as a shorthand typist and was accepted in the Inland Revenue Rating and Valuation Department whose offices were in the Old Schoolrooms, Broadgate in Lincoln next to the Duke of Wellington public house. (The site is now a car park). She stayed there for nearly five years until the birth of her eldest son, Paul, who was born in January 1959. Eileen remembers that "It was a wonderful friendly environment with great colleagues. I soon learnt where all the areas of Lincoln and the local villages were located. The staff were a very sociable group and George played in the Cricket team with them – once at Nottingham University".

They were settled into their Wellhead Lane home by the time Paul was born, and Eileen also found time to join the WI. It was at a WI Meeting in 1967 that Eileen's life changed and she has been kind enough to write this piece for this book.

"Early in 1967, Nocton WI had a 'round robin' asking members what improvements they would like to see happening in the village and the answers were given to the then clerk of the parish council, Mr Harry Jackson, who visited the WI and responded to the suggestions. After some discussion with members, Mr Jackson said that there was soon to be an election and asked if anyone would like to offer to be nominated. No one offered and the president, Mrs Phyl Redshaw persuaded me to put my name forward as there had never before been a woman councillor at Nocton. With the support of the WI ladies I received the second or third highest number of votes. I was pleased with my election and tried to bring forward improvements to the village including extra lighting, the footpath down to the Church from Main Street, the kerbing of Wellhead Lane, just to mention a few.

In particularly I remember the first chairman I served with, Mr Max Howard, who was in office until his death in June 1970. In those days the meetings were held in one of the outbuildings of Embsay House where we sat in comfortable leather armchairs or on the Chesterfield settee with a wonderful warm log fire burning in the huge grate lit by Mr Harry Jackson. Max Howard often came to the meetings in his carpet slippers and always had a friendly, warm presence. His love of Nocton was plain for all to see and he was sorely missed. During my 36 years as a parish councillor, I met many interesting people and my life was enriched by helping others. Our two District Councillors for many years, Bill Chambers and John Rose have been a great help to Nocton and never once refused any request for help regarding certain situations which needed attention at a higher level."

Eileen Moulds with her presentation gifts after serving for 36 years as a Parish Councillor - May 2004.

Eileen has and is still playing a leading role in village life. She was a member of the Nocton Friendship Club for over 30 years and Secretary until it ceased a few years ago. Both she and George prepared the Village Hall the monthly meeting for many years. George was also a committee member and vice-chairman and was a great help when Whist Drives were held for Club Funds.

Both of them have been involved with the Friends of Metheringham Airfield since it was formed 13 years ago as a tribute to those who lost their lives in the 57 planes which flew from Metheringham RAF and did not return. They both help at the Visitors Centre when it is open to the public and at functions. Eileen said that "Each year we are privileged to meet up with the members of 106 Squadron who return to the Base for a reunion. Very thought provoking"

Eileen and her grand daughter, Kate, helped with the Church Kneeler Project 2000.

Eileen is a member of the Nocton Village Trail Association and she and George helped with the Pebble Mosaic Path to the Church, which came second to Liverpool Cathedral in the 2005 Church Architects Award and she went with Cliff Baxendale to London to receive the Award. At the moment they are working on a Roman Pavement Mosaic which will be placed outside of the Old Row.

George spends much of his time tending the garden and playing Golf.

After an inspection of the new Church Path. L to r Chris Howard, George Moulds, Cliff Baxendale, Eileen Moulds, Cliff and Val's grandson and Val Baxendale. –July 2004

Eileen and George have four children and ten grandchildren.

Wellhead House was built by Mr Max Howard in 1936, it was designed by Ken Wood, who married Miss A.M. Howard in 1898 as recorded in the next section. Mr and Mrs Charles Suttle came to live here in the 1970's and became involved with village life, they both joined the Friendship Club and regularly attended church where Charles was an occasional organist for many years, his love of the organ started at an early age, for by the time he was 22 he had qualified as an Associate of the Royal College of Organists, his Fellowship came later. In 1935, Charles having left University with a degree in Electrical Engineering, came to Cranwell to the Education Department of the RAF. He served in Iraq, Baghdad, and then Aden where he met his wife Joan who was working with the Red Cross, she had come from India where she had cared for the POWs

from Japanese camps. They married in Aden in 1948 and returned to England in 1959, to RAF Locking and Charles was promoted to Group Captain and in the same year was honoured with an OBE.

He served at RAF Henlow, where he ensured that the Technical Cadets followed a three year degree course. At this time the new RAF Institute of Technology was planned for Cranwell and Charles later took up the post of Senior Director of Studies in the acting rank of Air Commodore. He retired from the RAF in July 1973

Group Captain Suttle, with wife and daughter after receiving his OBE

and then taught music at Sleaford High School for Girls. Joan served on the Parish Council for some years and she helped with the Library Trolley at RAF Nocton Hall Hospital. They celebrated their Golden Wedding Anniversary in May 1998. They found that Wellhead House was too large so they moved to a Bungalow in Scopwick to be nearer their daughter. Sadly Joan died in 1999 and Charles died in November 2003, leaving a son, daughter and two grand children.

A family photo at their Golden Wedding Celebrations.

Maybe it is near here that the Romans came to live. For one of their main requirements was a good spring of water that ran all the year around, and the spring in the nearby field does just that. At least two Roman coins have been found in the field to the west of this, plus some Roman roofing tiles, in the past five years. One must remember that the Railway was cut through here in 1882, which would most likely have disturbed the top soil and has caused the field to be divided into two.

We pass under the Lincoln to Sleaford railway line on our way to the cross roads. Here we will turn right to Nocton Rise and return to the crossroads to proceed up onto the Heath.

CHAPTER 5
History of the Howard family at Nocton
1742 – 1890

The Howards came to Nocton in 1742, and lived periodically at Nocton Rise. The house was originally only two storeys high and the extra floor was added later. The new front was added to the house about 1856, and since then they have lived in the house continuously to the present day.

Side view of Nocton Rise showing the older three storey farmhouse that faces South.

The first record of the Howards living at Nocton Rise is Lady Day 1750.

This is described in an Extract from Nocton Church Magazine July 1898

"The Howards have been farmers at Nocton for 148 years, - ever since Lady Day 1750, when Mr Edward Howard succeeded Mr Kent in the occupation of what was then the largest farm in the parish. It seems to have comprised 99 acres of which 37 were arable, with a right to turn out 300 sheep upon the open lands. Of the 5340 acres in the parish only about 840 were then enclosed, the remaining 4500 being open and uncultivated. It was in the following year, 1751, that Sir Francis Dashwood – who had married the widow of Sir Richard Ellis – erected Dunston Pillar as a lighthouse to guide travellers upon the roadless heath".

There is a letter that has been in the Howard records for many years. It is addressed from Nocton dated Nov. 11. to "My Dear Aunt," and it was "from your affectionate nephew J Robinson." The letter is about a vacant farm on the Wrest Estate and speaks favourably about the son of one of his tenants on Nocton Estate. "His name is Howard and his father and mother are

the old farmers of the real old stamp and are most respected people and excellent tenants." It has been deduced from other information in the letter that it was written in 1817 and the Aunt would have been Lady de Grey of Wrest and the writer was Frederick John Robinson whose wife had inherited Nocton estate the previous year, but we do not know if the tenancy was taken up on the Wrest Estate.

There is a Marble Monument to the Howards in the North Porch of the Church –it reads –

"In Affectionate Remembrance
Of Their Beloved Parents
Elizabeth Howard
Who died November 30th 1843
Aged 49 years:
And
Robert Howard, Who died July 6th 1858,
Aged 60 years:
This Monument is Placed Here By
Robert George Frederick And
Edward John Howard"

Extract from the Nocton and Dunston Parish Magazine – August 1877

CHAMPION RAM
Lincoln Longwool Sheep Breeders Association's
Annual Sale, 1938
Bred and Exhibited by E. M. Howard, Nocton

The Lincoln Longwool Sheep looked much the same in 1877 as they did in 1938.

"List of prizes from the Boston Show from the Lincoln Gazette. Lincolnshire Longwool Sheep. Mr Edward Howard won 1st prize for Class 22 - For the best 2 shear rams. He took several other prizes which are listed in the next section (The Heath)

The Lincoln Longwool Sheep looked much the same in 1877 as they did in 1938.

It was Edward Howard who had the front extension built onto Nocton Rise House. The stone was all selected and brought from the Ancaster Quarries by horse and cart and was completed in 1856.

Nocton Rise showing the 1856 additions on the right

Shows the older three story part of the house facing south with the newer extension, the front door of which, faces East.

E.J Howard and his wife with some of the family. A photograph taken about 1884, found amongst Kate Wright's (nee Howard) belongings at Winthorpe December 1960.

FROM THE 1890'S TO ABOUT 2000

The 1891 census states that Edward J Howard, aged 53, was living at The Rise with his wife, Eliza, and seven daughters. The eldest, Mary, was 26 and she was a Sick Hospital Nurse. Edith was 24, Katharine was 23, Alice was 21, Twins Eveline and Emeline were 11, and Nora was 6. They had a 40 year old Governess, called Emily Walker, who was born in Stamford, Annie Baumber was a housemaid, from Scopwick while Harriet Applewhite was the Nursery Nurse from Spalding and Sarah Finiral was the Cook and she had been born in Leadenham. All these people were living in the Farm house. John Pawson, who was born at Boughton and his wife, their two grown up children, a niece and two farm servants all lived in the Forman's House. George Richardson was the

Gardener and Groom, he was born at Kelsey, and lived with his wife and two young children in one of the properties at The Rise. William Turner, from Dunston, was the Shepherd, his wife and five children were living in another house and the residents of remaining property were Agricultural Labourers, John Flatters, born in Nocton and his wife Ann born in Market Stainton. The three sons of Edward and Eliza Howard were not living at The Rise on Census day.

To find out what the Howard family were doing during the last few years of the 19th Century some extracts from Church Magazines during 1898 have come to light and say:-

Thursday 6th January – Large and encouraging congregation met at Mr Drage's house on Mr Howard's Bottom Fen Farm at 7pm. The interest in these Fen gatherings seemed to decline during the summer, but it has revived again since the long evenings set in. The Vicar's expositions of Scripture have a great attraction for the dwellers of our Fen.

Our parish register for July records the marriage, in June, of Miss A. M. Howard with Mr K. Wood of Richmond in Surrey. Bride and Bridegroom have our best wishes for a long and prosperous and happy life! The great interest displayed in this wedding is only natural, having regard to the wide influence and general respect the bride's family enjoys not only in the parish but throughout the neighbourhood.

Alice Maud Howard and Kenneth Woods on their wedding day June 1898.

Edward J Howard and his wife, Eliza.

The Bride and Groom

Charles

On Midsummer Day, Canon Footman and Mr. E.J.Howard were re-elected to represent Nocton on the Nocton, Potter Hanworth and Branston Drainage Trust for the three years next ensuing.

A Sale of Work and Jumble Sale was held in the Vicarage gardens on 20th July. Miss Norah Howard helped with the Bran-pie. Charles and Miss Emeline assisted with the Weighing Machine. The proceeds were £24 17s. 10d. this was divided as follows:- £7 17s. 10d. for the Village Clothing Club and £17 0s. 0d. for the Home Missions.

And on the 30th July, the Nocton Lawn Tennis Club held their annual tournament. Miss Emeline Howard beat Miss H.M. Footman in the Ladies Handicap Final and C. E. Howard and Mrs M. H Footman beat H. G. Gambles and Miss Emeline Howard in the Mixed Doubles. On the 5th October, at the Annual meeting, a hearty vote of thanks was accorded to Mr Hodgson for kindly allowing the club the gratuitous use of his beautiful grounds.

Now a few extracts from the 1899 Church Magazines In the January magazine it was reported that the Misses Howards had decorated the pulpit in our beautiful church for the festive season.

On the 7th March, Mr Edward J. Howard took the chair of the annual meeting of the school managers. Mr. Bratt, the Head master, gave the attendance report for the year ending 28th of February, 49.5 being the average attendance.

And in December 1899, a small committee had been formed in Nocton and Dunston to make house to house collections on behalf of the Transvaal War Fund, for the relief of the widows and orphans of those who may fall while fighting our battles in South Africa. The Nocton collections are being made by Mr E.J.Howard on the Heath, Mr George Woolhouse in the Village, Mr Thomas Sewell in the Fen: and we understand that Mr.William Pepper and Mr. Harry Maltby are collecting in Dunston. The Rector felt sure that the response would be generous, and that he would be able to report the collection of a goodly sum next month.

We have not had access to all the church magazines, so there are many events that are not recorded in this book.

In 1911, Eveline Howard married Rev Frank Smith.

In the July1922 magazine, there is a record of the unveiling of a Memorial Window. 'There was a large congregation on Sunday, June 11th at the Evening

The Wedding of Eveline Howard and Rev Frank Smith in 1911

Service, when a new stained-glass was unveiled and dedicated by the Rev.R.Howard, Rector of Wilsford. It is the last of three on the North side of the Nave, and has been placed to the memory of Mr and Mrs E.J.Howard. This is expressed in the inscription, which runs – "To the Glory of God and in loving memory of Edward John Howard, for many years Churchwarden of this parish died July 4th 1914 aged 77 years; also of his wife, Eliza Anne, (daughter of the late Charles Ward, Esq., J.P.,Lincoln), who died October 1920, aged 79 years. During a long residence they took an active interest in this parish and were regular worshippers in this Church. This window was erected by their sons and daughters, June 1922".'

350a. 2r. 26p. paying a rent of £438 2s 6d per annum on a Yearly Tenancy. Nocton Rise was described as "A Capital Sheep and Corn Farm" including an excellent Farm House standing back from the road in pleasant grounds, containing Hall, Dining Room, Drawing Rom, Morning Room various Kitchens and Pantries, eight Bedrooms, Bath Room and Box Room. A Commodious Homestead including Stable for eight, Gear House, Chaff House, Barn, Granaries, Cake house, two covered Crewyards, Fowl Houses, four Crewyards with sheds, Cow house for two, Bull place, Loose Box, nine-bayed Implement Shed, Tool House, Meal and Boiling House, Carriage House, Saddle Room, Nag Stable for four, Granary and Wind Pump. Also, Foreman's and Stockman's Cottages. Nearby Two Pairs of Cottages each containing five rooms and outbuildings.

Charles E Howard

Information gleaned from the Particulars of the Sale of Nocton Estate in 1925, shows that Mr C.E. Howard was still a Tenant farmer, at that time, with

Charles E Howard's children, Roy, Molly, Joan and Max

Max Howard aged 2.

Yvonne Webber and Dinah 20th April 1932

There are many photos of the family at Nocton in the 1930's. By this time Max Howard was an agriculturist at the Lincolnshire Sugar Company's factory at Bardney, which had been opened in October 1927. The Motor Car was in its prime.

Preparing for a Sunday Picnic – July 1931

There were large family gatherings and friends came up from the village. This is shown in the photo of Dinah Howard and Yvonne Webber, for Yvonne was Herbert Dennis's grand daughter who was living in Embsay House at this time, with her parents, Annie and Leonard Webber.

It was on 19th April 1933 that Max Howard married Monica Newsum.

Max and Monica Howard on their Wedding Day – 19th April 1933

Rupert Taylor (Bestman) with Bridesmaids Mollie Battle (neé Howard) and Joyce Pumfrey

The best man was Rupert Taylor and their bridesmaids were Mollie Battle and Joyce Pumfrey. They toured the West Country for their Honeymoon going as far as Land's End and returning via the Wye Valley. They set up home in Wragby, and were both keen gardeners.

Max and Monica in their garden in Wragby – May 1934

We do not have photos of all the weddings but in 1938 Joan Howard and Fred Newsum (Monica's brother) were married in Nocton Church

Joan Howard and Fred Newsum's wedding in 1938

An another extract from the November 1944 Parish Notes

The Vicar had been absent from the Harvest Thanksgiving services through ill health. And he writes "I was not the only absentee. Mr Howard also was sick, and at the time of writing we are still anxious on his behalf. It is the more disappointing in that he fell ill again so soon after the very happy event, of the marriage of Dinah Howard to David Marshall on the 30th September, and Monica was the Matron of Honour. Something of pre-war rejoicing marked the occasion, and the bells sent out their peal of good wishes.

Dinah Howard and David Marshall's wedding, November 1944

And the following year, in June 1945 an extract from Nocton Parish Magazine about Max Howard's younger brother Roy who later spent his life in Kenya.

The War has become concentrated in the Far East, where some of our men have been fighting, under terrible conditions, for a long time. They have won a great campaign in Burma, and more help will lighten their burden. It was in the Burma campaign that Major Howard, leading his African Troops, won the Military Cross for gallantry, an honour that gives great pleasure to all Noctonians

All this time, Farming at Nocton Rise was progressing at a great pace, with the pioneering of the Sugar Beet crop.

Horse Hoeing Demonstration for Sugar Beet – 9ᵗʰ June 1932

There was amongst the Howard Family a member who was keen on Photography for there were many photos taken during the early 1930's as well as many taken around 1940.

"Bringing in the Harvest" 1940

"Harvest safely gathered in" Ricks all neatly thatched - 1940

Mr Lowis with a Coldrum Baler - Baling straw after threshing. - 1940

Land Girls loading mangolds tops for making silage -1940

Charles Howard was farming Nocton Rise at this time with the help of some Land Girls. Horses were slowly being replaced by tractors and in July 1949 the Rector, the Rev Kenneth Healy was pleased to record Mr Max Howard's success in winning the County cup for the best farm, together with the crop of prizes for Longwool Sheep. We are getting accustomed to his achievments at the County Show.

1940 - Steam Engine Demonstration – Mr Lowis from Branston

After the untimely death of Max Howard in 1970, an article appeared in the local press.

"Max Howard was a well respected man who gave a life time's dedication to Agriculture", and here is the piece that was written by Peter Scoley assisted by the Battle family and Mr C.L.Brembridge. It not only tells of Max Howard's achievements, but also what was happening in the Farming community at that time. It was entitled - The Great Agriculturist

THE Lincolnshire Show as we know it today owes a very great deal to the vision, hard work, and dedication of one man, the late E. Maxwell Howard, CBE.

Of course, he worked with the backing and help of other colleagues, but it was he together with Colonel Oliver Nelthorpe who foresaw the need to settle on a permanent site. The costs and difficulties of moving the show around the county were rising, and causing more and more problems. After much discussion and research (land in the Woodhall Spa area was considered, among others), the two men persuaded the council to invest money to purchase the land on which the Show is held today. Max, already Honorary Director, was appointed to carry on the office in the new enterprise. He accepted this daunting prospect, while a member of many other committees, as well as being on the Council and a steward of the Royal Show.

A friend and neighbour, when asked his views on the life and work of Max Howard, thought hard before replying.

"I think that of all the people in the county, he could be called The Great Agriculturist of Lincolnshire."

He then went on to quote the last verse of Kipling's "If", the first two lines of which read

"If you can talk with crowds and keep your virtue.
Or walk with Kings - nor lose the common touch,"

Another used the words "perfectionist and meticulous".

All these and many more in the same vein, helped to sum up the character of the man, show the respect in which he was held, and demonstrate the loss the county suffered when he died on the eve of the Show in 1970.

Max Howard was born at Moorlands, Branston, on March 28 1904, into a family long renowned for the excellence of its farming methods. A very famous flock of Lincoln Longwool sheep was kept, and later a highly respected herd of Lincoln Red Shorthorn cattle. At about the time of his birth, a near relative was busy instigating the formation of the Lincolnshire Farmers' Union, very soon to become the National Farmers Union.

On the retirement of his grandfather, his father moved to Home Farm at Nocton Rise, not without relief it seems. He had been given the tenancy of Moorlands on his marriage, but the land is not easy to farm, as the present owners know, and it must have been doubly difficult in the days when horses provided the only motive power.

Educated first at home, then Lincoln Grammar School and Haileybury, he returned to learn farming; formal agricultural training was a rarity in those days. Paradoxically, he did not show the care and meticulousness for which he was later to become famous, since, he recalled, he was always late for work, much to the chagrin of his father, earning many black looks and pointed comments from the staff.

Except for a period during the First World War, and shortly afterwards, farming had suffered a recession for something like 45 years. For long, people had been casting around, seeking alternative crops to grow, in order to increase profitability.

Unsuccessful attempts at growing sugar beet in this country go back as far as 1832: indeed there is an interesting quotation from the report of the United Kingdom Sugar Industry Inquiry Committee, 1935:

"During the 19th century, several efforts were made by individuals to establish a sugar industry in the United Kingdom; but in the absence of any State support they met with no success. Experiments in sugar beet cultivation continued, however, and from about the beginning of the present century, efforts were made by various bodies to promote the cultivation of the crop and the establishment of factories."

Needless to say, without the support of the people of this country they met with little success. On the Continent, however, different attitudes prevailed. The crop had been long established. Napoleon is said to have instructed scientists of the day to investigate its potential and plant-breeding stations in Holland, Germany and other countries had been flourishing since about 1860. European Governments have for a long time regarded farming in a rather more favourable light than had our own. To a degree this is understandable. We are an island race, a trading nation. They are part of a Continental land mass, and therein lies the difference. We have exactly the same problems today.

Perhaps the submarine blockade from 1916 to 1918 suffered by this country helped to push along the idea that we should not entirely rely on imports for our supplies. The crop was tried again in the south-eastern counties, this time with more success, and soon the idea was mooted to form the Lincolnshire Sugar Company.

Naturally, there had been other proposals, and much discussion. For instance, there was a proposal in 1909 to form a sugar processing enterprise at Sleaford. The estimated cost of the factory was £100,000 to process 500 tons per day, a colossal investment when compared with today's monetary values and factory input. After much effort, the Lincolnshire Sugar Company was formed on January 14 1927, with factories at Bardney in 1927 and Brigg in 1928. By this time sugar beet had been grown in the county for some years, but had been delivered to other factories.

Max was taken on as assistant to Mr Henry Beacon, the first managing director, and helped supervise the building of the plants. When operations began at Bardney in October 1927, Max became the agriculturist at Bardney factory. It would seem it is from this period of his life that the perfectionism began to shine through, according to the mass of documents he left behind.

Although sugar beet had been grown spasmodically for a very long time in this country, there was relatively little knowledge of the crop among the

Bardney Sugar Beet Factory - 29th September 1930

The Rail Flumes at Bardney – 6th October 1931

with the attitudes of farming in this country. To be fair, the slump was upon us, but it cannot be denied that those who paid attention to detail, came through that difficult time in the best way.

During 1936, the British Sugar Corporation was formed, and united what until then had been a fragmented industry. Obviously government was beginning to see the light. Max had held several posts on the agricultural side, while his friend, colleague and brother-in law Mr G. F. N. Battle, CBE (Eric to his friends), had been the senior contracts manager. Under the new regime they were both offered positions at the head office in London. However, by now Max was helping his father to run the Home Farm, on top of his other duties, and he declined the offer. Instead, he became the assistant contracts manager under Mr Swannack, leader of the party on the visit to Holland and Germany in 1930, who at that time controlled contracts at both Bardney and Brigg. Mr Battle, on the other hand accepted the offer, and eventually reached the heights of senior management, becoming Agricultural Director of the British Sugar Corporation. In 1939, Max became Factory manager at Bardney and held that position until 1945, when his father died. He resigned in order to take full responsibilities of the family farming.

farmers and processors in the country as a whole. It therefore soon became company policy to send fieldmen and agriculturists on as many fact-finding missions as possible. In 1930, a trip was organised for them to visit well-known plant-breeding stations in Holland and Germany.

Max has left a superb record of this outing. Thoroughly documented, though never published, it would be of particular interest to experts in the industry today; it is a textbook in its own right. Again and again, he draws attention to his admiration for the striving for perfection displayed, and one senses an impatience

Sugar Beet being loaded in 1942

Lincolnshire Sugar Stand at the County Show near Grimsby – June 1932, l to r H S Taylor, Mrs Taylor, W Swannack, E Marris, E Walter, J McCloy, Molly (Howard), J Chappell and Eric Battle.

So far, this article may seem to be a record of steady promotion and effort in a purely local affair. However, it must not be taken at face value. During these years, he had been travelling the country, lecturing on sugar beet growing, as indeed had many of the other executives.

Arthur Burnett Hoeing a Sugar Beet Seed Crop – 1ˢᵗ July 1942 (most likely being grown for Battles Seed Company in Potterhanworth)

Max was a member of a very large number of committees, some large and important, others small and not quite so important. Some were purely agricultural, some at local government level, both district and parish, others a diversionary nature like dances and ploughing matches, though still important in their own way in the social strata. He was a member of the wartime Agricultural Executive.

1947 Charles East - the shepherd with a lad chopping mangolds or sugar beet

But to each and every one, he could always be relied upon to give of his best.

It has been said that no one could put a person who had erred, in his or her place quite so politely as Max; indeed, some never knew they had been criticised, but, if the straying sheep did not return fairly quickly to the fold, the dismissal was equally polite and permanent. After his father's death the name of Nocton Rise famous for so long, continued to resound throughout the United Kingdom and such countries as Argentina and New Zealand, where many pedigree animals were required to enhance for bloodstock. Also, and the knowledge that he had gained was brought to bear. It was often said with grudging admiration that "No one could grow a crop of beet like Max"

Following the family tradition the NFU did not escape his attention. In the early 1950's he was elected chairman of the Lincoln branch and within a short time, the County – of course, the senior county branch in the country. Here again he left his mark, to the benefit of all members, and indeed those who were not, too. During his chairmanship he presided over the celebrations that marked the 50th anniversary of the formation of the Union, and may well have remembered an article in the NFU Record dated December, 1936, when a plaque was unveiled in memory of his father's cousin. Mr Ted Howard, the founder. On Friday, November 13, 1936, Max's father, in reply to a speech by a Mr George Gibbard, vice-president of the NFU, remarked that one of his earliest recollections of his cousin, then farming at Templebruer, was being accused, quite unjustly, of hiding the morning paper. Despite his protestations of innocence he received a spanking with a coal shovel, which he thought did more harm to the shovel than it did to him. Like others, he recalled the determined nature of Ted Howard, but after all, a man who could persuade farmers to launch a new idea like the Farmers' Union, and must have needed considerable tenacity and stubbornness!

Memories are notoriously short, and except for his contemporaries, I do not suppose there are many, who realize what Max did for Agriculture in Lincolnshire. But, for those interested, the number of Press articles, about him, or written by him is staggering. Even foreign papers feature often in his collection, as do records of the BBC broadcasts. The name of Nocton Rise had, at the time of his death, been well-known for years through out this country and latterly abroad. Year after year, prizes for sheep and cattle were won and exported.

RASE at Nocton Rise in May 1953

The 1953 Champion – Max Howard's comment on the back of the photo "Unbeaten at all shows"

Arthur Burnett – Head Shepherd

Max Howard with Frank Peel his Head Stockman and Norman Berridge his Under Stockman.

Sadly, today, the people of this country seem not to care for this kind of excellence, and his son Chris, the present treasurer of the Show Society, has found it impossible to carry on the tradition, though the spirit is not dead. Many other innovations have sprung, and continue to spring, from The Rise. Max, renowned for his administrative abilities, was also a well-known wit, and many people may have heard of The Dock Story. For years he had served on various committees with the late Ald George Flintham, MBE, my father's partner. Uncle George was always very proud of his

early potatoes, of which he was the original grower in this part of the world and a specialist. He was also inordinately fond of a herd of Lincoln Red cattle he had, and it was his greatest pleasure to drive round at least twice every day to observe progress. One year was a particularly good one, and during June he decide to invite all his friends to have a look around, and show them what really good farming was like. This was before the days of spraying. The potatoes and cattle were a picture, and not a weed was to be seen in the corn crops. The invitations, or rather the commands, were issued for a Sunday visit. Now Max knew of Uncle's foibles, and thought of a plan to pull his leg. He was a very fine amateur gardener, and his knowledge of plants was unparalleled. On his farm was a wood in which massive docks thrived. He went along, picked out the largest he could find and placed it in a very big plant pot. Next, he rang my father, told him of the plan, and the two conspirators were next seen in huddled conversation in the corner of a bar of a local pub, one moment in serious conversation, and then convulsed with laughter. The great day arrived, Uncle, all unsuspecting made his usual rounds early in the morning, and made home for breakfast. Father, who lived nearby, had been watching, having risen at an unusually early hour for a Sunday morning, telephoned Max and reported that all was clear. Max seized the pot, ran out to his waiting car, and hared off to Martin Moor, where he carefully placed the gigantic weed right in the middle of the best field of barley on the farm. At about 10 o'clock, the guests began to arrive, and soon the convoy set off for the treat. Most of the land described is no more, having been engulfed by airfield construction during the last war, but was, in those days, black acidic moorland, ideal for growing early potatoes. The motorcade pulled up alongside the fields of fine crops, bordered by birch and oak trees in full leaf, underneath framed by rhododendrons of all hues in full bloom. Patiently, the assembled friends listened to a harangue on how to grow potatoes, dug a "cooking" when invited, and retired perspiring to the cars. Further down the road, the guests were proudly shown lovely crops of barley and wheat, growing on the less acidic land. Suddenly, one of the passengers in my uncle's car exclaimed:-

"A saay George, I thought yer said y' adn't got a weead on th' plaace"

"I 'aven't," was the reply.

"Well, what's that bloody greeat dock doin' in the middle o' that theeare clooase then?"

"Wheeare?" asked uncle explosively. The offending piece of alien herbage was pointed out to him.

"Well dang me!" explained uncle. "It wasn't theere this mornin' 'cos I was round at seven."

He stopped the car with a jerk, which nearly caused a multiple pile-up as the following cars had to take emergency action, opened the door, and strode off across the field. On arrival at the site of the dock, he was seen to take off his cap and jump on it. Purple faced, he replaced his headgear, picked up the dock in its pot, and walked purposefully back to the column of cars. He stood looking at them, searching the eyes of every member of the party. Finally, looking both Max and my father straight in the eye he said, "If I 'iver find out who did this, I'll wring the buggers' necks!" The remainder of the tour was, of course, enjoyed by everyone, except that uncle got his own back, he made sure that the most colossal party developed back at The Grange, and every person present either received a real old - fashioned telling- off from their wives for being late home, a hangover that lasted for at least 36 hours, or both. He never knew for sure who had played the trick on him, but of course he had very strong suspicions.

Max was, for many years president of the Lincoln Fatstock Show, and when this was disbanded, he became the first president of the Lincoln and District Agricultural Dinner.

Max after receiving his CBE with Monica at Buckingham Palace

He was a self-taught authority on gardening, antique furniture and Wines.

During the last few years of his life he gained the distinction, on top of everything else, of being asked to be the Agricultural Adviser to Ministers of Agriculture, Fisheries and Food, on behalf of six counties. He held this post until his death. The tragedy came on the eve of the County Show in 1970, and the stunning shock rocked everyone. Indeed, I believe there was talk of cancellation, but by then, of course, things had gone too far. In any case, he knew he was desperately ill, and it was his wish that, the Show must go on.

The Lincolnshire Agricultural Society's showground has developed in a way in which I am sure Max would have given full approval, and will remain a permanent memorial to the Great Agriculturist of Lincolnshire.

The Rev Crampton wrote in the Parish Magazine after the burial of Max Howard on 26th June 1970. "The Bishop of Lincoln in his funeral oration paid an excellent tribute leaving me with little to add. For my part I was much encouraged by his faithful attendance at Holy Communion at All Saints Church and also for his advice, always offered in a spirit of kindness and never in criticism at meetings of the Nocton P.C.C. The advice was always good and expressed his life long knowledge of the village."

Lincolnshire Show and the Howard family

Edward Howard was a Main Steward for 20 years from 1870.

Charles Howard was Chairman of the Stewards from 1932 to 1939

1939 Lincolnshire County Show at Grimsthorpe Castle, Bourne. H,R,H, The Duke of Kent, Charles E Howard Esq. Lord Willoughby d'Eresby

1955 Royal Show in Wollerton Park, Nottingham. Max Howard, H.M. The Queen and the Duke of Portland.

Max Howard was an Honorary director for 15 years, and then Show Chairman in 1970. He was responsible for assisting the Lincolnshire Agricultural Society in finding their permanent home at Grange-de-Lings.

Chris Howard was elected to the society council in 1965, has served on the executive for fourteen years and has been chief steward of catering and treasurer and he became President in 2004.

2004 Lincolnshire Agriculture Show June 23rd and 24th - Princess Anne talking to Robin Battle and Chris Howard, who was the President.

Robert Howard is the present generation that is assisting with the running of the show.

Lincolnshire Agriculture Show June 16th 1957. "After Tea in Fred Townsnd's Caravan"

When Chris Howard was asked to write a few words for this book, he willing wrote 'a few words' - a modest few words for someone who has played such a large part in this village and the surrounding area.

"My older sister and I and my parents moved to Nocton Rise in 1939 to join my Grandparents. We were brought up in Nocton Rise, living there with my Grand Mother and Father until they died.

I remember the War Years as generally cold and dark as we had no electricity until 1947, not much heating and no help for my mother (who is now 96 and living in a flat in Lincoln). There was a family gathering in 1947 at Nocton Rise, this photo shows l to r Roy Howard, Agnes (Mother of the Howards present) Eric Battle, Fred Newsum, Max, Molly, Joan, Di, and

Monica with Maureen and Christopher at Nocton Rise 1941

Family Gathering 1947 – L to r. Roy Howard, Agnes Howard (Max's mother), Eric Battle, Fred Newsum, Max Howard, Molly, Joan. Dinah, and Monica

Monica. Both my sister and I went away to school (when I was 6 in 1945) and I came home and started work when I was 17, Caythorpe Farm Institute at 19, and got married at 24, moving to Ram Farm which had been Robert Wright's Farm, at that time tenanted by Derrick Young, the ex Nocton Manager. I lived there for 12 years (and bought the Farm in 1992) and moved to Nocton Rise in 1975.

Chris with his father at the Lincoln Red Shorthorn Show on the Carholme April 1953

The next generation of Breeders of the Lincolnshire Longwool Sheep, about 1960

Pea Vining

The Howard family attending a friend's wedding in 1959

I helped form Branston Potatoes Ltd (now Branston Ltd) and Branston Engineering Ltd – the latter moved from Mere Road Branston to Grange Lane Nocton in 1995. I became chairman of both companies in 1988.

When I started farming at Nocton in 1956, we had some 23 men and women on 440 acres – now we have 3 or 4 times the acreage and just 3 men. In those days, we had Lincoln Longwool Sheep, Lincoln Red cattle, Large White Pigs, 1,000 Battery Hens, a few Tractors, some Horses and our first Combine Harvester capable of harvesting 200 acres.

Now the Livestock has all gone.

Beet Harvester – revamped by CENH.

We have less Tractors but their horse power is up by eight times, we still have one Combine Harvester but it can do eight times as much.

1980's Charlie Burnett on Claas Combine

Chris Howard taken in 2000.

I joined Farming at the start of a 'Golden' age which finished in 2000 with Sugar Beet and Barley the main crops, changing to Oilseed Rape, Winter Wheat and Potatoes.

Now, regrettably, by order of the Government the main crop is 'Set Aside' and 'Conservation', perhaps with the oil crisis, crops such as Oilseed Rape will return as it is used in many fuels.

I have been very happy to have lived in Nocton and have spent 'time' on the Parish and Church Councils, having been the latter's Treasurer for 40 years and Churchwarden for the third time. I am pleased that my eldest son, Robert, is now carrying on, also very happy to have three grandchildren living in the Parish as well as another five nearby."

Nocton Parish Magazine – May 1965
Baptism on April 18th Alice Mary Howard.
The Vicar, the Canon F. Burrows, wrote "Four Generations – it was a great joy to see Mrs. A. M. Howard amongst our communicants in our Church on Easter Sunday after her long illness, and I know that it gave her much pleasure to be able to remain in the church for the Baptism of her great granddaughter, Alice Mary, the infant daughter of Mr. and Mrs. Christopher Howard. Two more of Mrs. Howard's five great grandchildren were amongst those who attended the Baptism, so it was a delightfully family occasion on which we received the daughter of our Parochial Church Council Treasurer into the wider Family of Christ' Church.

AND SO THE NEXT GENERATION IS HITTING THE HEADLINES

July 2002 saw Robert Howard pick up Tescos "Best Spud Farmer Award". Robert impressed the judges with the high quality of the farm's potatoes as well as his willingness to try new varieties and growing techniques and his environmental and conservation activities. He puts the success down to 250 years of farming experience, his father's concentration on the potato production after the war and his four full time staff who understand the countryside. He grows 70 hectares of potatoes on the 650 hectare farm and has recently installed their own warming store at the farm because potatoes are stored cold, but can be easily bruised if handled at less than 5C. Robert is also the Chairman of the Institute of Arable Crop Research Centre's PCN link project, which is currently trying to find ways of treating eel worm infestation of potato crops without using chemicals.

Robert Howard

CHAPTER 6
Moving up the Heath

And so we leave Nocton Rise and return to the Cross Roads. Charlie Burnett, one of ten children, was born at Temple Bruer in 1920, and the family moved to Nocton Rise seven years later. At 14 years old he started working full-time for E.M. Howard and continued until he was 70, seeing many changes, from horses to high tech machinery. Elsie was born at the Mere in 1920, being the youngest of ten children. The house on Lincoln Road, Nocton was especially adapted for the large family and is now two semis. Elsie Spurr worked at The Rise as a Nanny where she met Charlie and they married in December 1941, and Charlie moved into number 7 where they lived until 1997.

Charlie and Elsie had long associations with the Church and in October 1966, Charlie was admitted to the office of lay reader and preached in many of the local churches as well as being a church warden for Nocton. The following year Elsie was introduced to the Mothers Union by the Enrolling Secretary, Lizzie Jackson. In June 1985, Charlie was presented with his 50 years agricultural service medal, by Princess Anne at the Lincolnshire Show. He died in January 2001, and was buried in Nocton attended by his many family and friends and it said that he was a straightforward master craftsman, who was much liked and admired by all who knew him. And in 2003, Elsie passed away, having been a member of the MU, and the Friendship Club for many years.

The Grange Farm is the first farm that we come to heading west up the Heath. The earliest record about the Grange comes in the Lincolnshire Museums booklet about the Nocton Park Priory, as the Lands at the Grange were part of the Priory land. But we are not going back that far.

There is a Sale Advert (Without a year) "To Be sold by Auction, on Saturday the 7th of April at Nocton Grange, the Farming Stock Belonging to Dr Willis". He had 4 Cows, Several young beasts and about twenty Horses. Three Waggons, three Broad-Wheel Carts, Ploughs, Harrows and other Utensils. This is the Dr Willis who treated George III in his later life for madness.

In 1872, George Woolhouse is recorded as farmer of Grange Farm. And he is still there when the 1901 Census was drawn up. But before 1923, Mr C

Featherstone had moved to the Grange, because an extract from the May 1923 Parish Magazine records the death of Mr C Featherstone. For many years he had been in indifferent health, as was the case while he resided at the Grange Farm on the Heath. We believe the last thing he did before leaving was to present the village with a large flag for the flag mast on the Village Green.

When the Dennises bought the Estate, they must have taken Grange Farm "back in hand" as only the Homestead and Buildings are mentioned in the Sale Particulars of 1925 and it is not included in the Schedule of the Estate as Occcupied.

Nocton Grange - A description from the Sale particulars of The Nocton Estate dated July 1925.

Nocton Grange taken in the 1940s sent from Anthony Walledge

Nocton Grange was a half timbered farmhouse standing in pleasant grounds, and containing five bedrooms, bath room, W.C., attic, Drawing Room, Dining Room, Business Room, Kitchen, Scullery, Dairy and Cellar.

Homestead included Nag Stable, Trap House with Granary over, Boiling House, three Crewyards with open Sheds, two Loose Boxes, Piggery, Fowl Houses, Coal House, seven-bay Wagon Shed, and a Wind Pump.

Also Two pairs of Modern Cottages each with five rooms. (These are still standing on the Roadside).

Nocton Grange Early 1960's

Chris Howard had a letter from Anthony Walledge in 2005 enquiring about state of the Grange for he had been born at there in September 1936 when his mother and RAF father had rented rooms there, and he sent a photo from his family's photo album. He also mentioned that the parents of Jim Broadbent (the actor) were also lodging at the Grange in the 1940's.

The Glossop family were the last residents of the Grange Farmhouse before it was pulled down by Smiths Potatoes in the 1960's. George died in 1955 aged 76. He worked on the estate for 45 years and was an expert drillman.

George Glossop in his later life

The Farm buildings were upgraded and used for pigs. Described in the 1975 Sale by Private Treaty (Strutt and Parker) as "The modern specialised pig buildings comprise environment-controlled Weaner House about 123 ft. by 24 ft. with 30 pens with automatic drinkers and slurry disposal. Stone and concrete block with a slate roof. Mill and Mix Shed with grain store. Two Pig Fattening Yards, each 135 ft. by 45 ft, overall, built of breeze-block and steel frame with asbestos roof with automatic feeding troughs, Nine pens and lean-to straw storage area. Two Offices. Brick, concrete frame and Yorkshire boarding with asbestos roof Piggery, about 162 ft. by 60 ft. overall, containing 36 weaning pens, 1 Farrowing House with 10 crates, Sow House with 84 cubicles and 7 boar pens.

Now Branston Engineering use the Buildings for their Workshops.

Heathlands Farmhouse is not mentioned in the 1925 Sale particulars, so one must assume that it did not form part of the Estate in 1925, and it was renamed Pawsons by Smiths Potato Estates because Mr Pawson had lived there and by 1975 there was only a Barn with 11 bay Lean-to Implement Shed.

Heathlands Farm House – also pulled down in the 1960's

Traction Engine helping to bring in the 1946 Harvest at Pawson's Farm, Nocton Heath

Harvest 1946. With the Second World War over the labourers posed for this photo at Pawson's Farm.
L to r –Fred Robinson, Fred Worrel, Alf Saunby, Percy Etheridge, John Robinson, - , Dennis Wass, Wilf Hubbard, Ernie Dickinson, and Harry Franklin, with Bill Watson on the Engine.

The Dennises and then Smiths Potato Estates farmed the Heath as a whole unit so it is difficult to identify the location of each photo.

Fred Glossop working with Horses

"Taking bags of corn to the Station"

Alf Sleaford on the Traction Engine

A picture of young Joe Topham was taken about 1925 in one of the farmyards up on the Heath. Joe was one of the few servicemen who did not survive the Second World War.

Joe Topham in about 1925

Ram Farm

Information gleaned from the 1891 census refers to Nocton Heath where Robert Wright, aged 73 and his wife, Sarah, aged 71 lived with their two sons, Robert, 36, and William, 32. Also living in the house were three Domestic Servants, five Farm Servants and two Irish Shepherds.

The 1901 Census states that Robert Wright, Farmer, lived on Bloxholme Road. The other residents included a Housekeeper, a visitor, and five Servants including a Groom. In the cottages lived a Foreman, Cattleman and a Shepherd.

A report from the Parish magazine states that "Mr Robert Wright was married at Portsea, on Tuesday the 2nd of October 1901, to Lizzie Bailey, and the happy event was celebrated by the merry pealing of the Nocton Bells during the afternoon. The bridegroom gave a Tea at five o'clock at Mr Gresham's, the Red Lion, Dunston, to his workpeople, the Choir, Ringers etc. We take this opportunity of wishing Mr and Mrs Wright a long and happy life in Nocton."

Mr Robert Wright died in December 1933 and his widow and daughter donated a Memorial Screen in the Church to his memory.

Fred Robinson at Ram Farm

Approaching Ram Farm taken in 1986

Front of the House

Soon after this Mr Derrick Young (Manager of Nocton Estate) took over the running of the farm until the 1960's when he went to live in Potterhanworth and E.M. Howard Ltd then took over.

From Ram Farm you can see Dunston Pillar. This is an extract from Country Life September 28th 1901.

Nocton Hall lies 3¹/₂ miles west of the old coach road from Sleaford to Lincoln and in the old times, was in a region infested by highwaymen, who stripped the traveller of many worldly goods as he passed that way. It was easy at night to miss the way altogether, and therefore, in 1751, Sir F. Dashwood built the only land lighthouse that exists in England. It is known as Dunston Pillar, and is 100ft. high, having now on the top a statue of George 111, which replaced the lantern in 1810, and was placed there to commemorate the monarch's Jubilee. The distance from Nocton Hall to this notable pillar is about three miles. In the "Journal of Agriculture," 1843, Mr. P. Pusey made some remarks about the land lighthouse - which, we may remark, stands on the summit of Lincoln Heath - that deserve to be quoted here: "This Dunston Pillar did appear to me a striking witness of the spirit of industry, which in our own days has reared the thriving homesteads around us, and spread a mantle of teeming venture to its very base. And it was certainly surprising to discover at once the finest farming I had ever seen and the only land lighthouse ever raised. Now that the pillar has ceased to cheer the wayfarer, it may serve as a beacon to encourage other land owners into converting their dreary moors into similar scenes of thriving industry". The dwellers of Nocton Hall were interested in the raising of the pillar, and were concerned largely in the improvement of the land thereabout.

Dunston Pillar at the turn of the previous century with Eustace Pask and his infamous Game Cart.

We now move onto Glebe Farm. When the Heath was enclosed, a certain percentage was given to the Vicar as part of his income and his area was called Glebe Farm.

An extract from the Nocton Parish Magazine dated June 1900 about The Late Alderman Glasier J P.

George Glasier, who died at Orchard House, Lincoln, on Saturday the 24th of March, 1900; was born at South Hykeham on the 11th day of September, 1807, and came to live on Nocton Heath at Lady Day, 1810, when his father John Glasier, became tenant of Nocton Glebe Farm. Only the other day he was describing to the writer the delights of his childhood at the old farmhouse, where Mr Melbourn's foreman now lives: how the old vicar –Mr Curtois – used to ride over from Branston to look at the game-birds, which the Glasiers kept for him, and choose which of them should be sent to Lincoln to take part in the fight at the cock-pit in the yard of the old Reindeer Inn, where the Lindsey Bank now stands: and how the vicar – Mr Hobart – took no delight in such old-world "sport", but gave his father notice to quit that he might let the farm to Mr Gambles: how Lord Buckinghamshire used to shoot "no end of pigeons" from the square pigeon-cote that stood about fifty yards to the south of the old farmhouse : how in that terrible winter of 1814, they had to dig the sheep out of the snow by the Fox Covert, and the hares, made bold by hunger, came up to the buildings and ate oats from the sacks in the barn : and how he himself used to trudge in all weathers down the coach drive to Miss Brackenbury's school against the church. (He was born in 1807, so this is the old school in some cottages opposite the present school and the church was demolished to make way for The Ripons church). He could not remember the name of the people at the "Rice" – the Howards were in the village – but John Dawson was at the Grange; and Mr Wright's grandfather, at the top farm, lent Mr Glasier horses and wagons when he had to move to Rand. The family was very sad at leaving, and Alderman Glasier, the other day, at the age of 92, could not quite bring himself to forgive the "new Vicar" for giving them notice to quit.

By 1925, the Glebe land no longer belonged to the Church for it was in the ownership of The Dennis Estate Ltd., according to the Sale Particulars, Glebe Farm consisted of a Commodious Stone built farmhouse containing seven Bedrooms, WC., two Sitting Rooms, Kitchen, two back Kitchens, Pantries and Outbuildings.

The Homestead (chiefly converted as accommodation for pig herd) included :- Trap House, Coach House, three Loose Boxes, Saddle Room, Granary, Pigsty, range of Pigsties, Trap House with Pigeon Loft over, Coal House, Fowl House, Chaff house, Four Crewyards with Sheds, two Pigsties, Six Loose Boxes, two Cow Sheds, Granary, Barn, eight –bay Implement Shed and Wagon Shed, Clipping Shed, Stable for 12 and three old Cottages. This must have been one of the largest farmhouse and homesteads on

Katherine Wright (Neé Howard)

the Estate, but by 1975, there was no Farmhouse and a few buildings:- A 2-Bay fertilizer Store, 2-Bay Tractor Shed, 3-Bay, 4-Bay, and two 6-Bay Implement Sheds, a 6-Bay Shelter and Yard, Barn and Store.

Lincolnshire Longwool Sheep thrived on the Heath and were famous worldwide. And there must have been a lot of rivalry between the Heath Farmers for the "Best Ram" or the "Best Pen of 5 Ewes"

William Wright

1890's - The Nocton Heath Lincolnshire Longwool Sheep Breeders

An Extract from a Parish Magazine - A Flock of Sheep being sold for £30,000.

Nocton Heath was famous for its Lincoln Longwool Sheep and Lincoln Red Cattle. The names of Casswell, Dean, Howard and Wright were as well known in the world of South America, South Africa and on the Continent as they were in Lincolnshire. Early in this century a flock of sheep founded in 1790 on Nocton Heath was sold to Buenos Aires for £30,000.

And here is another Extract from the Nocton and Dunston Parish Magazine – August 1877
"List of prizes from the Boston Show from the Lincoln Gazette.

Lincolnshire Longwool Sheep.

Class 21. – For the best shearling ram; 2ⁿᵈ, £10, Robert Wright, Nocton Heath, Lincoln; 3ʳᵈ, £5, Ditto. Highly commended, Robert Wright and Edward J Howard, Nocton Rise, Lincoln.
Class 22. – For the best two-shear ram, 1ˢᵗ, £10, Edward J. Howard, Nocton Rise, Lincoln.
Class 23. – For the best three-shear or older ram, 1ˢᵗ Robert Wright, Nocton Heath, Lincoln.
Class 24. – For the best pen of 5 ewes, having suckled lambs up to the 10th July, 1877. Reserve, E.J.Howard, Nocton Rise, Lincoln.
Class 25. – For the best pen of five shearling gimmers, 3ʳᵈ, £2, Robert Wright, Nocton Heath, Lincoln. Highly commended, Thomas Cartwright, Dunston Pillar, Lincoln. Commended, Edward J.Howard, Nocton Rise, Lincoln.

Under the Heading of "Sheep" it goes on to say – In the classes for Leicester sheep the competition was limited, and it is a question whether it is worth the while of the Society to offer prizes for a breed which finds but scant favour in this county. No less than 300 animals competed for the handsome prizes offered for Lincolnshire long-wool shearling rams, the whole of the honours being divided between Mr.A.Garfit and Mr. Robert Wright. The former gentleman, who was first and second at Liverpool, was first and fourth here, but, curiously enough, ……………to be continued (and we have been unable to find the next piece!!)

One must remember that these sheep were not transported by lorry, they would have travelled to Liverpool by train on the "Liverpool, Manchester, Sheffield, Lincolnshire Line". The Lincoln to Sleaford Line was not opened until 1882.

The Boston Show, run by the Society, would have been the annual Agricultural Show. At this time, there were two Agricultural Societies - Lincolnshire South and Lincolnshire North, they amalgamated soon after this date.

Mrs E Bradshaw wrote a letter to the Lincolnshire Life in September 1983, stating that her father, Aaron Clarke, had married in Market Rasen in 1898 and then moved to the Woodside on Robert Wright's Nocton Heath Farm to set up his first home. This lady was born in 1899 and has lived in many homes in Lincolnshire and was writing from the The Rest Home in Heighington. Her father became a well known cattle dealer and bought Lincoln Longwool sheep from Mr Wright, which were often sold and shipped out to Buenos Aires in Argentina. It was in 1922 that Aaron went out to Argentina to visit his sister who lived a few miles from Buenos Aires.

1950's - The Nocton Heath Lincolnshire Longwool Sheep Breeders

Sheep breeding carried on into the 1950s, and nowadays sheep are bought in at about 5 to 6 months old and fattened on the sugar beet tops during the winter months.

We now return to the Village via the Old Carriage Road that begins at Dunston Pillar and finishes at the Hall, following in young George Glasier's footsteps. Parts of the road can still be used as a Public Footpath.

CHAPTER 7
Time passes at the Top Lodge

Imagine that it is 1873, the year that the Earl of Ripon surprised everyone by resigning as Lord Lieutenant of North Riding and from his position in the cabinet, and you are the Coachman returning home after a long journey having driven down the carriage road from Dunston Pillar. You know there is not much further to go. For there is the familiar sight of the Top Lodge with the two Griffins holding the Coat of Arms, on the Gate Posts, with the Lincoln to Sleaford road passing right outside.

Top Lodge

Detail of Statues on the Gate Posts

The Griffins are holding the Marquis of Ripon's shield between their paws, which measured 5 feet high and 3 feet across. This shield depicts 'stags at bay' with a central smaller shield embossed with the Royal Coat of Arms, of three rampart lions, a harp and two roses. You look to the left and there you see the new Church Spire, and further to your left, on a little hill, stands the Windmill with its four sails going around. It had been standing there since 1833 when it replaced an earlier

The Windmill

one (built about 1827) which had been destroyed by fire. The miller was Mr Thomas Geenfield, who was born in Glentham and he lived in the village with his wife Ann, who was born in Gainsborough. According to the 1891 Census, Thomas was 71 and his wife was 65, and they lived in a cottage next to the Vicarage, with their elderly servant Sarah Wilson from Thimbleby and 17 year old George Codling who was a Miller / Journeyman. There was a field opposite the Windmill which rejoiced in the name of "Tin and Bottle Field", where the village people dumpt their tins and bottles, before there was a Council refuse service.

We will move on about 30 years to 1907, and standing in much the same spot, 50 yards west of Top Lodge, you will see and hear the changes that have occurred in that elapsed time. First you will hear an unfamiliar sound, you look over the wall on the left hand side and there, in a cutting, are two rails with a steam train approaching, making for Nocton Station, which is further down the line on the right hand side of this bridge. For in 1882 the Lincoln to Sleaford Railway line was opened which made a huge difference to Village Life in Nocton, more about that later.

Second, you look to your left, yes the Church spire is still there, but we are led to believe that the windmill was taken down about 1902. From the 1901 Census, we learn that 45 year old Charles Greenfield was living near the Vicarage. He was described as "own occupation" and Miller and Baker, his wife Susanna had been born in Bucknall and their eldest three children had all been born at Chapel Hill, whilst their three year old had been born in Nocton. Living with them was a young man by the name of Fred Tye, 21, who originated from Moulton and was also described as a Miller and Baker, and two servants. John Philips, 16, from Metheringham and Alice Pilsworth, 13, from Dunston.

And thirdly, there is Norman Hodgson coming towards you in his new motor car, so your days as a coachman are numbered.

1907 Rover similar to Norman Hodgson's Car

People are still talking about the report in the December 1898 Church newsletter, about a fatal accident "We are sorry to have a record of a fatal accident that took place about 4pm on Tuesday the 1st of November in Mr Clifton's field opposite Nocton Mill. John Caunt and John Pilsworth, both of Dunston, were engaged in getting stone for road making; contary to their instructions they were undermining – instead of removing the top – when nearly two tons of earth fell in on Caunt, crushing him instantly to death. The Vicar, Mr Joseph Roberts and Mr Woolhouse, (from the Grange) were soon on the spot, but there was nothing to be done beyond removing the body to Dunston; an inquest was held on the following Thursday, resulting in a verdict of Accidental Death, with a rider that the deceased ought not to have been undermining. Much sympathy is felt for his widow and children."

Another 30 years have passed by. Coachmen have long gone. But standing in much the same place, you

will see a two foot gauge railway track coming up on the right hand of the carriage drive. The right hand gate post has been removed to allow both vehicle traffic and the light railway line to pass through. And there is a Level Crossing gate, which is operated by a man, who cycles from the station to open and close the gates, as and when required.

Light railway crossing B1188 Lincoln to Sleaford Road

This photo was taken in November 1932, showing Ivy and Mrs Blakey, with their bikes, waiting at the crossing. Don Turner was on the Engine and Bill Jackson was the Guard. The bike lying against the wall belonged to the man from the station. To your right you will see a large building which is "The Mill" for the Estate.

Yet another 30 years have past and it is 1968. There is no sign of the Estate Light Railway, this was removed a few years earlier. The Griffins have also disappeared from the top of the gate posts. Now there is a large Fowler Steam Powered Road Roller helping to construct a new piece of the B1188 Lincoln to Sleaford road.

Fowler Steam Powered Road Roller

Constructing Nocton bypass

This section of new road was being built to cut out two railway bridges and three right hand bends. The Local Press reported of the opening of the road in August 1968 along with some pictures.

"Easier Run From City to Sleaford
A new section of road along the B1188, which runs from Lincoln to Sleaford, was opened on Tuesday morning. The road, half of which has been paid for by British Rail, has cost £46,000.

First cars to use the new bypass

The new section has been built between Branston and Nocton to replace a dangerous part of the old road which contained two U-bends, and an unsafe railway bridge.

As British Rail would have normally had to pay £22,000 to bring their bridge up to regulation standard, they decided to pay this amount to the Kesteven County Council to go towards a new by-pass road. The County Council approved of this scheme, as it would eliminate the two dangerous U-bends.

A spokesman from the Council, said that it is hoped in the future, that more alterations may be made to the road as many parts of it are potentially dangerous. Nothing is programmed, yet, however. Because of weight restrictions which have been placed on the railway bridge in the last few months, the Lincolnshire Road Car Company has had to divert its buses through the Smiths Potato Crisp's farm yard. This has meant a quarter of a mile's uncomfortable riding for passengers and a lot more wear and tear on the buses.

Now, however, it is hoped that the buses will be able to use the new stretch of road once permission has been granted by the Traffic Commissioners."

Now in 2007, and one would think that the road layout had always been as it is now. Mr. & Mrs Clark have erected two stone pillars for the drive to his house, which passes over the railway bridge, past the Top Lodge, and down the 'Avenue' of Lime, Oak, Ash and Sycamore Trees, some of which would have been planted during the time that the Ripons lived at the Hall.

Aerial View of the Village and RAF Nocton Hall taken in 1983.

CHAPTER 8
"The Railways"

We now have to make a decision - Left to the Village or Right to the Station.

We will go right and return to the village in a little while. The Railway Station was an important part of Village Life. It enabled ordinary people to travel – there is an account about the 1898 Church Outing to Ipswich and Felixstowe on a specially chartered train.

Nocton Station

Hickson's the Coal Merchant

Coal wagons came into the Station, and discharged their load. S.A.Hicksons & Son were the Coal Merchants who bagged up and delivered the coal to the villagers' homes. There is a photograph of Fred Hickson with the Train Driver and the Station Master.

Potatoes and other farm produce would have been delivered to the station during the time that Norman Hodgson was running the Nocton Hall Estate and especially during the First World War.

When Messrs Dennis bought the Nocton Estate in 1919, they were already familiar with growing

Fred Hickson with Train Driver and the Station Master

potatoes and using a light railway on their estate at Deeping St. Nicholas. So within a year they had laid four miles of track on the Fen around the Wasps Nest area and horses were used to pull the trucks. During 1920, a complicated Agreement was made between W.Dennis and Sons, Ltd., and the Great Northern and Great Eastern Joint Committee. Under this agreement the Committee at their own cost constructed Sidings at or near Nocton Station, this Agreement was dated 31st December 1920. So the "Railhead" was established with a siding for loading into railway trucks. At about the same time, the concrete corn mill for storing and grinding corn and making up the cattle rations was built, as well as the Maintenance Sheds, Engine Shed and Bag Store.

In the 1925 'Particulars of Sale' brochure, under Nocton Station it reads "The Estate Warehouses and Workshops including Railway Shed, about 80 ft. by 65 ft. A Building, about 246 ft. by 65 ft., containing Implement Store, Garage, Workshop and Store. Engine House, Mess Room, Clearing House, Petrol

Store and Loading Dock, with convenient Sidings and Yard." There were also some Special Stipulations about the use of the light railway for the forthcoming harvest and about the agreement between the GN&GE Joint Committee, these are printed out in the Appendix under Chapter 8.

The Light Railway and the Main Line from the top of the Grain Store.

Mr J. Herbert Dennis purchased the estate from his father's executives, and now that most of the farms on the estate were being farmed 'in hand', it was soon realised that an efficient means of transport was required to bring goods to the Station area from all corners of the Estate. At this time, there were over 200 horses being used on the farms. The Estate Agent, Major Webber, soon set about purchasing and then installing more track, about 30 miles in all, of 2 ft. gauge railway. This was laid radiating from the 'Railhead' to the Heath and the Fen, the farthest point away was in the North East at the Bardney Sugar Beet factory when it was opened in 1927. A Gantry was built with a mechanical grab which lifted the sugar beet across the river to the factory. Rolling stock was required. The locomotives were bought new, but the wagons were ex-army, and were converted for the Dennises requirements in their Maintenance Workshops within the complex at the Railhead. Conversions were carried out on Wagons for carrying bags of potatoes, and grain, Guards Vans with letter boxes, Water tankers for both domestic water and

water for the steam engines – both ploughing and threshing, and bogies for moving the track around to the different fields in the Fen.

The farm was run on military lines – there was a large map of the whole Estate at the Mill, the fields, roads and especially the railway were marked on it. The railway was run by a traffic controller, who was in charge of allocating the train drivers and guards to the trains and wagons to carry out their various duties. Coal was transported down to the Pumping Station by the River Witham. The light railway was an integral part of "The Shoot". A regular timetable was kept – a small boy's dream!

When Herbert Dennis died in 1936 the Nocton Hall Estate was purchased by the Estates Company and the farming enterprise was called "Smith's Potato Estates, Ltd.," and they carried on with the same tradition of using the Railhead as their headquarters.

The Station was closed in 1963/4. But the line is still open and the nearest station is Metheringham formerly known as Blankney.

Station House 1996

The Station Master's House and the Station Yard were sold in the 1970's and this is now a small industrial site.

The Mill

Frank Smith with the Directors and Factory Managers

Taken sometime between 1936 and April 1946 in the Smith's Potato Estate yard outside the Workshop.

Frank Smith - seventh from the left in the front row, and fifth is Cyril Scott. Top left is Mr Robertson the Nocton Fen Manager who lived in Park Farm House and Mr Burton is standing between Frank Smith and the Manager of the Lincoln Factory on Newark Road.

CHAPTER 9
Smiths Crisps

SECTION A) THE LIFE OF MR FRANK SMITH, WRITTEN IN THE 1970'S.

Frank Smith was the brain child behind the "Crisp".

Frank Smith

He had been a journeyman grocer – who, in 1919, did not enjoy good health – and was an employee of a wholesale grocery firm who manufactured a small quantity of crisps and the production was his responsibility. Seeing the great possibilities of the potato crisp, he asked his employer for permission to increase production but the employer said "No". So Frank Smith therefore handed in his notice and in 1920 with the financial aid of three or four friends started producing crisps with a staff of eight in a disused building in Cricklewood, North London. For some time Frank Smith was his own Manager, Salesman and Traveller and in the early days sales were not too good. Then he had an inspiration – why not put a wisp of salt in the packet? He did, and from then the firm never looked back – more staff were engaged (school boys and girls used to wrap the salt packets on Saturdays), salesmen were engaged to search for business, van drivers for deliveries, and other factories were opened and the business grew and grew until in

1929 a Public Company was very successfully floated to be known as Smith's Potato Crisps (1929) Ltd., which today (1970) has a staff of 600 employees within the Sales and Distribution Department alone. There are seven factories, including the Newark Road, Lincoln Factory, and depots in England, Jersey, Australia, Holland, France and producing a high grade crisps from the most modern machinery. How different to the days of 1920 when the potatoes were sliced by hand.

In addition to all its factories and subsidiary companies, the Company wholly own an agricultural estate of some 7,500 acres at Nocton, near the city of Lincoln and here about one-tenth of the potatoes used in the manufacture are grown. The purchase of this Estate in 1936 was made through the far-seeing eye of Frank Smith who visualised using his own grown variety of potatoes for his crisp manufacture and having a stock on hand for an emergency.

Opening Village Hall October 1946

Frank Smith took a great interest in the Nocton Estate - both agriculturally and socially. Both he and Mrs Smith encouraged their staff to enjoy their leisure time, for they were both present at the opening of the Nocton Village Hall in October 1946.

A photo taken in 1954 shows Mr and Mrs John Ireson with Mr and Frank Smith and the following year Frank Smith celebrated his 80th Birthday on April 5th 1955.

Frank Smith retired in September 1955, and when he died the following year, a piece was written in the Nocton Church Magazine.

Mr and Mrs John Ireson and Mr and Mrs Frank Smith in 1954

Mr and Mrs Frank Smith on his 80th Birthday

"A Good Friend to Nocton". Mr Frank Smith, managing director of Smith's Potato Estates, Ltd., (Patrons of this Living), until his retirement in September 1955, died at his home at Osterley on December 28th, aged 81 years. Mr Smith was a real man, who had a very great quality of courage. His energy, strength of purpose and assiduity made him a great leader. This 'real' man had a kindly humour, a strong sense of sympathy and a big heart that guided his sympathy and made him the kind generous, fair and just man by which the world knew him. He paid many visits to Nocton and it was his joy and pleasure to travel round the Estates watching the various farm operations and to see the fulfilment of the vast scheme which he, through foresight and courage had initiated. His death is the end of a great epoch and the loss of a guide, philosopher and friend. our deep sympathy is extended to his dear ones in their sorrow.

Section b) Chitted Potato to Potato Crisps

Potatoes have played an important role on Nocton Estate since the time that the Hodgsons grew extra potatoes during the First World War, then the Dennises made their fortune from the humble "Spud", and now Smiths Potato Estates have taken over the Estate to grow their special crisping varieties. In the early 1950's potato production was the first consideration

on the Estate and about 1,000 to 1,400 acres are annually devoted to this purpose, with an average yield of 8 to 10 tons per acre depending on conditions. The special varieties known to make the best Crisps only are grown, mainly from seed purchased from Scotland or once grown on the Estate. All seed is chitted in boxes before planting. The harvesting of this potato acreage averaging over 10,000 tons is a heavy task, involving the organisation and handling of gangs of casual labour in the autumn and the potatoes are then placed in "A Potato Clamp or Pie" until they are riddled (sorted) and bagged up ready to be sent to the customer, who maybe a wholesaler in London or a Crisp Factory anywhere in the Country.

This collection of photographs was taken in the late 1950's.

Ian Spafford unloading chitted potatoes ready for planting.

Bill Franklin driving the Fordson Tractor planting three rows of potatoes.

Dib Tindall with horse and cart collecting the potatoes from the potato machine pulled by a Fordson Tractor with a very early canvas cab.

R Brazier and F.Worrell putting the finishing touches to a quarter mile long Potato Clamp or Pie.

T Flintham, G Baxter, and P.Ward riddling potatoes.

THE SMITHS GROUP MAGAZINE—April, 1965

OLDE HUMBLE POTATO

I arrive in a sack
Treated gently at that,
For no bruises or cuts
Can I bear.
I'm well washed and scrubbed
In an electric tub,
Then drained of water
Till I'm bare.
With others I go
Into a Hopper you know,
Then up a moving chain
To get spun then sliced,
Tossed like a dice into Oil.
Quite refreshing and so
Being tossed and flipped
To the end of the fry, ditch, and
On to belt, to go
All shaken and shook
I'm blown down a duct
To a bag all crinkly and cold.
I'm packed in a box
With a seal on the top,
For there's no escaping you know.
My appearance has changed
Yet I'm still the same
As the potato of days of old.

GEORGE,
Boilerman.

George the Boilerman from one of the Crisp Factories wrote in the 1965 Smiths Group Magazine this poem about the Crisp

Loading potatoes onto the Light Railway.

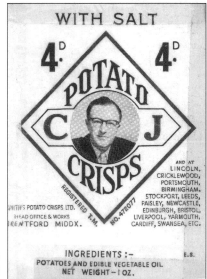

A 1956 Bag of Smith Potato Crisps

Bags of Potatoes being loaded onto a lorry by A.Bee, P.Bell and R.Duckering.

October 1970 saw the launch of the Beef and Onion Flavoured Crisp.

CHAPTER 10
The arrival of Mr John Ireson and Farming in the 1950s and 60s

Derrick Young was the Manager for the Estate from 1936 until he retired in 1946, when Mr John Ireson took over the duties of General Manager. Much was written about the Smith's Potato Estates at Nocton in the early 1950's. Stanley Farmer wrote an article for the Power Farmer in January 1951, in which he says that the critic would, no doubt, be inclined to dismiss the Smith's Potato Estates, at Nocton, in Lincolnshire, as a "factory farm". But this would be telling something less than half of the story. Certainly on this 8,000-acre estate, which produces nearly 10,000 tons of potatoes every year for the Smith's Crisp factories, a measure of factory scale planning and organization is inevitable. But the Nocton estate remains essentially a farm, and Mr. Ireson, who is the general manager there, retains the outlook of the farmer rather than a factory manager. A glance at the cropping programme soon reveals that the primary objective of growing potatoes has not been allowed to lead to an unbalanced farm policy. Well over two thousand acres of wheat are grown every year, over 700 acres of sugar beet, about 500 acres each of barley and oats, and smaller acreages of peas, kale, swedes and other crops. The potatoes now have indeed to take their turn in the four-year rotation, though Mr. Ireson admitted that circumstances occasionally compel him to "slip in an extra crop here or there". The land, too, is well stocked, with between five and six hundred Lincoln Reds, some 700 pigs, chiefly Essex, nearly 2,000 sheep and well over a thousand head of poultry all help to maintain balance and fertility. The small T.T. herd of Dairy Shorthorns is being slowly built up; and awards, which include the 1949 Silver Medal for the highest average Shorthorn yield in the county, provide evidence of how well this is being done.

Smooth running of the farm programme depends on the solution of the twin problems of transport and labour distribution. With the 300 permanent labour staff employed, balance must be held between a heavy call on casual labour at peak periods and long, semi idle periods during the slack months. The story of the farm is, in fact, bound up with the way in which these two problems have been tackled." And the article goes on to talk about the light railway, all the tractors and machinery, also the machinery repair shops housed in an old aeroplane hangar at the Railhead. There is a staff of forty with nearly £8,000 worth of spares in stock, for planned maintenance and any unforeseeable emergency. Here practically any service or repair job can be carried out. Besides the repair shops for implements, tractors and the rail engines there is a welders' shop, with facilities for oxy-acetylene and electric welding, carpenters' shop and stores. Carts, trailers and railway wagons are made in the workshops, also some of the many tractor cabs used on the farm.

Lewis Hemming with his son Fred in 1950

This photo shows Lewis Hemmings and his son, Fred, in the wheelwrights' workshop in 1950.

Sidney Redshaw

An extract from the October 1949 S.P.C. magazine, shows a photo of Mr Sidney Redshaw, who was a life-time agriculturist, having been employed on the Estate at Nocton for 28 years – for the first twelve as a farm worker and then for sixteen years as foreman. Being a man of simple tastes, his only hobby appears to be looking after machinery and attending ploughing matches. He looked back on his visit to Head Office for Mr Frank Smith's 70th Birthday Party as one of his most interesting experiences. His daughter was also employed on the estate. As a relief to farm duties he liked nothing better than motoring to the seaside.

A Brochure was prepared in 1953 for the purpose of giving the Shareholders of Smith's Potato Crisps, Ltd., some information about this great farming enterprise. A Copy of this is in the Appendix under the title "Shareholders - 1953 Brochure"

In 1946, Smith's Potato Estates, under the leadership of Mr and Mrs Ireson, provided three large Village Halls. One in each Nocton and Dunston and one at Wasps Nest. Each hall forms the centre of the community's social life, and, indeed, it provided facilities lacking in many villages of comparable size. Nocton Village Hall has a licensed bar which fully compensates for the lack of a public house in the village. Mr Ireson was also keen on the workforce having formal 'get togethers' as can be shown by the photos of "The second Staff Dinner in January 1954"

Jan 1954 2nd Staff Dinner

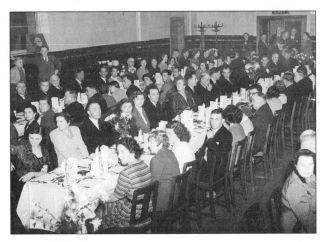

Jan 1954 2nd Staff

George Chambers worked and lived on the estate all his life and was Senior Foreman for Nocton Fen from 1946 until he retired in 1965. Rod Hargreaves joined the company in 1959 as Farm Manager and held the position until his retirement.

It was in April 1962, that the Mayor and Mayoress of Lincoln, Councillor and Mrs Herbert, accompanied by the City Sheriff, Mr B.Clarke, and the Sheriff's lady, Mrs Clarke, visited the workshops, mill, corn dryers and toured the Estate. Mr. J. B. Pettigrew, the Lincoln Factory Manager (Smiths Crisps on Newark Road), was also in the party. The Mayor, who is an engineer, was extremely interested in the workshops and the machinery, and he saw the blacksmith in action and various machines being repaired

1962 - Mayor and other members of the Party watching a horseshoe being made by Frank Merryweather

The Photo shows Mr B.Taylor, Mr J.B. Pettigrew, Mrs Clarke, Mrs Herbert, The Mayor and the Sheriff watching Mr Frank Merryweather make a horse shoe.

1962 - Mayor's visit in April

This photo shows the Works Foreman, Mr Ingall and Mr Ireson discussing a point with the Mayor in one of the Workshops.

It is amazing that by 1963, all the horses had been replaced by a fleet of sixty tractors, thirteen combines, pick-up balers, a fleet of lorries, sugar beet harvesters, mechanical potato planters and other modern machines, which had made the Estate fully mechanised. The light railway had been taken up and some twenty miles of roadways made, enabling potatoes to be loaded direct from field to factory. Two corn dryers had been erected which, with the storage capacity of the Mill, could hold 4,500 tons of grain. But there was still a Wheelwright working on the Estate. Now almost extinct, pushed out by this mechanical age, Mr Fred Hemming was still working and shown

A view from the top of the Mill – Thirteen combines in the Yard waiting for the signal to go out and harvest the corn.

Lorry drivers, S.Smith and A.Bee with their 12 ton Albion Lorries outside the Estate Workshops.

here making a cart wheel. He was the senior Estate Joiner and Wheelwright, having been taught by his father the late Mr Lewis Hemming. The wheel he had just made was for the carriage which carried the metal pipes for the Irrigation system used on the Estate to help the crops grow better in a dry season.

Fred Hemmings with a Wheel 1965

Each year there was a Staff Dinner usually held in January or February and there were many photos taken "On the Night", however some of Mrs Ireson's collection do not have a date and are being included here.

Left to Right – Ron Brummitt, Rod Hargreaves, Ernie Turner, Ann Hargreaves, John Davis, Elaine Hay and Peter Hay.

Mrs Ireson talking to Albert Ingall.

Rod and Ann Hargreaves with Mrs Bury (Mrs Ireson's Sister) and Mr Annersly.

At the Staff Dinner in 1962, Mr Cyril Scott, Managing Director, told his guests and staff that the Estate was one of the largest farming units in the country, and it had set an example in mechanization. He went on to say that 'The Estate was primarily used for potatoes, and he felt that after 40 years experience of using them, that Lincolnshire grew some of the best potatoes, and that they used about 1,700 tons a week for crisping.' These potatoes were transported all over the country, hence so many lorry drivers at Nocton. He also said 'Potatoes should be handled as carefully as eggs. They should not be dropped or roughly handled, as a bruised potato made a poor Crisp.

Later, the Managing Director presented the awards, we happen to have a photo of the Lorry Drivers who were presented with their long service awards.

Mr Scott and Mr Ireson with the Lorry Drivers who received their awards

There is a Table of Directors, Head Office, Factories and Depots at the end of 1962 and this is in the Appendix under Chapter 10.

1963 Annual Staff Dinner

Back Row l to r Rod Hargreaves (Farm Manger), John Saul (Member of Shoot and Farmer), Bob Bowser (Member of shoot and Farmer), Cyril Scott, NFU Man, Factory Assistant Manager, Mr B Pettigrew (Lincoln Factory Manager), Peter Alsford (Estate Stock Manager), S.Treavatt (Office) and John Ireson (General Manager) One of the standing ladies is Mrs Pettigrew. The Ladies seated l to r Mrs Saul, Mrs Alsford, Mrs Bowser, Mrs Scott, Mrs Ireson, Mrs Hargreaves and Mrs Treavatt.

Staff Awards at the 1963 Staff Dinner

During February 1965, at the 13th Annual Staff Dinner in the Canteen of the Lincoln Factory, Mr L.A. Baker, a retired Lincoln Banker said that "The coming to Lincolnshire of Smith's Potato Estates had been 'a godsend' to the County" and Mr Cyril J. Scott, the Managing Director of the Smith Potato Group, replied by saying, "We have heard of competition, but we do not take any notice of it. Smith's first made potato crisps in this country, we built up the trade and we intend to retain that trade". Mr Scott then made a presentation of a gold watch to Mr John Ireson who was retiring on the 31st March, after nineteen years as general Manager of the Nocton Estate, and to Mrs Ireson a gold wristlet watch.

Mr John Ireson receiving his gold watch from Mr Cyril Scott, February 1965

He also presented watches to Mr A.E.Bee and Mr G.W.Petch to mark their 25 years' service on the Estate. Up to this time eighty one watches had been presented to employees who had worked on the Estate for 25 years. Then the following lorry and van drivers who had driven during 1964 without an accident received cheques from the Company and awards from the Royal Society for the Prevention of Accidents.

A. E. Bee	Third oak leaf bar to 10 year medal.
L. Jackson	Second oak leaf bar to 10 year medal.
E. Brookes	Ten year medal.
F. Redshaw	Third bar to five year medal.
H. Gash	Second bar to five year medal.
R. Ball	First bar to five year medal.
R. Blackburn	Third year certificate.
A. Horton	Third year certificate.
G. Towns	Second year certificate.

And so, on 31st March Mr John Ireson retired from being General Manager of the Smith's Potato Estates. Mr Hargreaves presented "A Brace of Silver Pheasants" to him on behalf of all the employees on the Estate. At such a time, an appreciation is written about the person or people concerned, this piece has come from the April 1965 edition of the Smiths Group Magazine

Mr Hargreaves presenting Mr Ireson with a brace of silver pheasants from the employees, on his retirement.

Mr and Mrs Ireson at their farewell luncheon at the Savoy Hotel in April 1965

"He came to Nocton from Holmewood in Huntingdonshire where he was Resident Agent on an Estate of 7,000 acres and in addition, he managed properties in London and Yorkshire for the same owner.

During Mr. Ireson's management there have been big changes on the Estate - the tractor, combine harvester and the giant corn dryers have superseded the horse, sail reaper and the threshing drum. The light railway has given way to new internal roads and lorries. New methods are employed for pea, sugar beet and potato harvesting, indoor stores for ware and seed potatoes are replacing the potato clamp and glass chitting houses. The irrigation scheme to take water to part of the Heathlands has recently been completed, one could go on and on.

Over the years Mr. Ireson has become well known in Lincolnshire and in his public work has been a County Councillor, District Councillor, member of the Kesteven Agricultural Executive Committee, member of Drainage Boards and Chairman of the County Council Farm Institute Committee.

In the villages, Mr. and Mrs. Ireson have been connected with the activities of the Village Halls and Sports Clubs and Mrs. Ireson has increased the social life by, to mention a few items, socials, bingo, whist drives, beauty queen competitions, Christmas festivities and over the last two years has formed the Dunston Over Sixty Club of which Mr. Cyril J. Scott is president. Mrs Ireson has been President of the Nocton Women's Institute since its inception in 1946, was a Founder Member of the Dunston Women's Institute and for some time acting Enrolling member of' the Dunston Mothers' Union. She has also been very interested in the Church and Chapel Sunday Schools at Dunston. At Embsay House many Fetes and Garden Parties have been held and the Children's Sports which she started in 1947 have become an annual event."

A few days later the Directors of Smith's Potato Estates Limited gave Mr and Mrs Ireson a special presentation luncheon at the Savoy Hotel in London. Tribute was paid to Mr Ireson's work on behalf of the Company for so many years, and also to Mrs Ireson's outstanding contribution to the social life in the villages of Nocton and Dunston.

Summer 1962, the Annual Outing, the children and their mothers with a few fathers are waiting for the bus to take them to the seaside for the day.

CHAPTER 11
Nocton Estate from 1965 to 1995

1st April 1965, Jim Smart and his wife took up residence in Embsay House. Mr Smart carried on with the improvements that had been started by Mr Ireson and Mrs Smart soon realised that there was a need in the village for a Club for the "Over 60" section of the community, as there were now 83 people living in Nocton who qualified for such recognition. As Mrs Smart had had previous experience in setting up this type of club she was asked to be the leader. And so "The Friendship Club" was formed and thirty five villagers attended the first meeting on 12th July 1965.

Mr and Mrs Jim Smart being introduced at the 1965 Annual Staff Dinner by Mr and Mrs Ireson.

On the Farming Front, the staff numbers, and consequently the houses and cottages, were being reduced from the 300 that were employed in 1946, down to about 150 in the late 1950's and early 1960's, it was during this time that many of the Heath and Fen houses were demolished for they required so much modernisation that it was not economical to spend money on them, and more workers came into the village to live, either in the newly built council houses or the modernised Estate houses. So in 1970 only 100 people were employed and most of them were in Estate owned houses.

The improvements to the insulated temperature-controlled Potato Store continued and by 1967 the building was extended to twice its original size. This building and all the elaborate equipment that it contained was designed to ensure that the potatoes were delivered to the factories in perfect condition for crisp manufacture. By 1970, the five storey Mill had changed it use from storage of grain, corn drying and dressing and crushing, mixing and processing foodstuffs for the different kinds of livestock, to just storage purposes and grinding ratios for the pigs. The Pigs were kept in purpose built piggeries at Grange Farm. Only a few Cattle were left on the Estate with last leaving in 1979. The corn drying was handled by two plants which, together with storage buildings, were situated in the Workshop Yard. The Workshop continued to play an important part in the running of the Estate, here a large range of spare parts were kept with a staff of men including the Foreman, Storekeeper, mechanics, carpenter and bricklayers, all of them responsible for the maintenance of equipment and repairs to the properties. There was also a well equipped four wheeled drive mobile workshop that could travel to any part of the Estate to deal with repairs on the spot. There were numerous vehicles operating on the Estate. 65 tractors together with supplementary equipment, such as trailers, foreloaders, hedgecutters etc., there were ten combine harvesters, five potato harvesters, six sugar beet harvesters and five pea viners as well as ten lorries and seven Land Rovers which were continually on the move over the network of the roads that traverse the Estate. During this time there were about 100 staff employed, this included four in the Office, with Mr Bill Chambers as Manager

Smiths Potato Estate new office block

The Team in the Office – Mr Bill Fenner, Mr Bill Chambers, Mr Jack Eagle and Mr Stuart Flynn.

The four Section Foremen – l to r - Mr Jim Houseman, Mr Bill Watson, Mr Bill Woodhead, and Mr Fred Gash.

and Mr Jack Eagle, Mr Bill Fenner, and Mr Stuart Flynn. The Farm Manager was Mr Rod Hargreaves, and under him came the Foremen for the four farming sections – Mr Fred Gash being in charge of Nocton Fen Section A and Mr Bill Woodhead of Nocton Fen

Mr Jim Smart and Mr Rod Hargreaves, the Farm Manager, discuss the next job to be done.

Section C (don't know what happened to Section B!) while Mr Bill Watson was responsible for the Heath Section and Mr Jim Houseman for the Middle Section. The Potato Manager was Mr Robin Dant, the Potato Store Foreman was Mr Ken Sharpe and the Workshop Foreman was Mr David Shaw.

The Farming Policy 1971 to 1975.

THE FARMING POLICY

(a) **Arable:**
The estate is situated in an area producing good yields and the variety of soil structure permits flexibility so full advantage can be taken of market conditions.
The cropping during the last four years and for next season is as follows:

	1971	1972	1973	1974	Proposed 1975
Potatoes	797	591	410	404	420
Sugar Beet	870	859	869	874	1,000
Peas	931	1,398	1,461	1,237	1,250
Wheat	2,679	2,468	2,836	2,786	2,570
Barley	1,131	1,071	757	988	1,010
Grass	74	98	137	192	230
Kale etc.	34	42	46	39	40
Fallow	12	3	2	–	–
	6,528	6,530	6,518	6,520	6,520

Basic Potato Acreage 1975 – **465 acres.**

The Estate was bought by an American company, General Mills in 1971, and their English Agricultural Section was known as Tom Foods and by 4th June 1975, with completion two months later, the estate had changed hands again, being bought by the Guardian Royal Exchange, who had an agricultural subsidiary called British Field Products A new farming company, Nocton Farms, was established to farm the land. It is from this sale that we can glean much information about the estate and village in 1975, as "A Sale Particulars Brochure" was produced. Embsay House, 65 dwellings, buildings, farmland and tracks amounted to 6719.846 acres and there was 435 acres of Woodland. There were 6 vacant cottages and 36 cottages let mainly to retired employees at a peppercorn rent, some of these only had a W.C. and no bathroom as late as 1975, and two small farms in Dunston let to tenants, being 65 and 23 acres respectively. Also 3.795 acres at Nocton Village Hall and Recreation Ground, also Dunston Recreation Ground of 6.627 acres, both of these were let to Parish Councils on a 30 year lease which commenced on 25.3.73. The Brochure goes into great depth about each field, with O.S. Ref and acreage, while each set of Farm Buildings are well described. The Limestone Quarry on the B1188 had recently come in hand.

From this one can see that the potato acreage had halved in five years, but the increase in sugar beet was about 20% and peas by about 25%.

There had been many improvements to the field system in recent years with many dykes having been in-filled and piped with hedges removed to make large enclosures, some as large as 200 acres. This of course allowed larger machinery and less men to produce an increased harvest.

There are not many records of the following few years, but when Mr Jim Smart retired on the 8th December 1980, after 15 years as General Manager of Nocton Farms there was a Presentation Evening in Nocton Village Hall.

December 1980, Mr Jim Smart receiving a retirement present from Mr David Bridge

Over a 100 people attended to hear Mr Bill Chambers introduce Mr Rod Hargreaves the Farm Manager who presented Retirement presents to Mr Fred Woodhead (Table Lamp), Mr Bill Turner (Wall Clock) and Mr Frank Tomlinson (Shooting Stick). Mr Chambers then introduced Mr David Bridge the new General Manager of Nocton Farms Ltd, who presented a wall clock to Mr Jim Smart. Mr Smart was then asked to present Gold Watches for 25 years service to Mr Dick Ball, Mr Dixie Blackband, Mr Albert Green and Mr Peter Gash. Safe Driving awards were presented to Mr Dick Ball. Mr Dixie Blackband and Mr Les Jackson.

Mr David Bridge moved on in May 1985 to be the Managing Director for the whole of British Field Products based at Weasenham Manor in Norfolk. Mr David Ellis took over the position of General Manager of Nocton Farms and during his time in office saw Royal Insurance acquire the Estate.

In January 1989 there was another presentation of long service awards when long standing workers at Nocton Farms were given a special mark of appreciation when they were presented with gifts for a total of 160 years with the company. The four men - Peter Chapman, Bill Chambers, Jim Hardy, and Eric Hardy had each notched up 40 years of work and were treated to a celebration supper. Among the guests were the Chairman of British Field Products, the parent company - Alistair McCorquodale and his wife Rosemary, and the Secretary of the company, Roy Towler and his wife who had traveled from Norfolk for the occasion. Employees along with their wives and girlfriends gathered in Nocton Village Hall for the presentation.

January 1989 another long service award ceremony - l to r - Bill Chambers, Jim Hardy, Alistair McCorquodale, Rosemary McCorquodale, David Ellis, general manager, Peter Chapman, David Bridge, managing director and Eric Hardy.

It was on Wednesday 28th November 1990 that Nocton Farms held another long service award presentation evening in the Nocton Village Hall. Over a hundred people attended the proceedings when a cold supper and wine was served before the awards were presented. Mr Ian Green and Mr Trevor Green (twins) and Mr Frank Dawson all received their 25 years service watches. The twins came to Nocton Farms as students, and their status was never changed and as they are both still employed on the farm this must be one of the longest training sessions ever!!. Both Mr Derek Sellars and Mr Brian Woodhead received their 40 year tankards. Mr Ken Baines received a carriage clock for his retirement and all the residents of Nocton Village and employees of Nocton Farms wished him a happy retirement.

It was in 1995, that Royal Insurance put the whole of the British Field Products empire onto the market, all 19,051 acres. By this time there were 77 houses on Nocton Farms Estate, of which nine were vacant and twenty three let under various tenancies and only forty two were occupied by farm and estate staff.

Mr and Mrs Paul Clarke bought the Nocton Estate on 1st December 1995..

CHAPTER 12
Down to the Big Wood

The woods have always played an important part in the life of Nocton Hall Estate, for both timber and shooting. The Estate has been reputed to provide some of the best shooting in Lincolnshire.

From the 1891 Census there were two gamekeepers, Henry Curtis, aged 51years who was born in Pocklington, Yorkshire and Charles Chanty aged 35 years who was born in Croxton, Leicestershire. Henry's wife, Mary, was 49 and she also was born in Pocklington, at this time she was looking after Marie Bearpark, a 12 year old 'Boarder' who had been born in York. Charles' wife, Eliza, was 24 and born in Bottesford, Leicestershire. Within 10 years there had been changes for by 1901 Kenneth Dykes was described as a Gamekeeper with a 24 year old 'Boarder' called Tom Traines who had been born in Helmsley in Yorkshire. Soon after this Census George Stiff came to work on the Estate. From the turn of the century to 1919, the bag at Nocton averaged 10,000 birds in a season – 4,000 Pheasants, 4,000 Partridge and 2,000 Duck. One of the farms down on the Fen is called Decoy Farm, so one must assume that there was a duck decoy in that area. Then the land would have been drained to grow potatoes for W. Dennis and Sons for the number of ducks shot during the following few years dropped dramatically.

Information gleaned from the 1925 Sale Particulars, shows that the woodlands extended to about 472 acres and were stocked with Oak, Ash, Conifers and Underwood, and placed to hold a good head of Game. In Nocton Wood there was a pair of Keepers' Cottages, with stabling and kennels, and in the Top Plantation, up on the Heath, there was a stone-built five roomed cottage.

Gamekeepers' Cottages

Aerial view of Gamekeepers' Cottages

The Underwood would have been covered with bluebells and lily of the valley during May. People came from far and wide to see these flowers and to pick the lilies of the valley and the money would go for charity usually Lincoln County Hospital. This went on for some time until Mr Dennis found out that they were being sold on a Lincoln Market stall and the practice was stopped.

An extract from the Chronicle dated 12th October 1940 – A Venerable Couple Who Saw Many Changes. A venerable Lincolnshire couple, Mr and Mrs George Stiff, of Nocton celebrated their golden wedding on Sunday, but the male partner in the alliance was confined to his bed, owing to temporary indisposition. Nevertheless, a quiet family reunion took place. For 31 years, Mr Stiff was the head gamekeeper, retiring five years ago. He was the son of a farm bailiff, he was born at Erswell, Suffolk on 11th August 1869, and his parents paid twopence a week (old money - 1/120th of a pound which is less than one new pence) for his schooling. When he had just turned ten years of age he commenced work as a gamekeeper for sixpence a day. In 1899 he moved to Toddington, in Bedfordshire, where he was gamekeeper for the late R.S.(Bob) Sievier, the famous race horse owner. It was March, 1904, that he moved to Nocton as head gamekeeper to the Hodgson family, who on leaving Nocton, presented Mr Stiff with a handsome cheque as a mark of their esteem. When he retired in 1935, he was again the subject of a presentation, receiving an autographed silver salver and a cheque. George Stiff prides himself as a partridge driver. "I could drive 'em through the neck of a bottle" he told the reporter with a merry twinkle in his eye. Although he did not himself mention it, the reporter was told that he had received the highest compliments from many people on his skill in this direction. His record bag of partridges is 222 brace in one day and of pheasants 1,127. He averaged ten thousand head of game each year during the time he was "in harness". It was in October 1890, that he took Betty Gasking, a native of Ixworth in Suffolk, for his wife. Mrs Stiff, who was born in 1872, has brought up a family of nine – six sons and three daughters. Five sons served in the Great War (WW1), Charles Thomas attained the rank of sergeant in the Lincolnshire Regiment, and is now head gamekeeper at Nocton, taking over the position on the retirement of his father. Percy George served with the mechanical transport in eleven different countries, and now (1940) drives a Lincoln Corporation Bus. Another son, Cecil Gascoine, was also a sergeant in the county regiment and was three times severely wounded, losing his left leg. He was awarded the military Medal for bravery in the field. At the present time he is caretaker of the Ruston Works canteen in Lincoln. Archer Alfred, a lance corporal in the Lincolnshires, was killed in France in 1917. Gordon Arthur, another son, served in France with the Lincolnshire Regiment and the West Yorkshires, and was wounded. He is now a sergeant in the Lincolnshire Constabulary, stationed in Stamford. Of the daughters, Daisy Edith lives in Grantham. Another married daughter is Kathleen, whose husband, Mr A.E. Young, is a keeper on the Nocton estate, Lily May is also married and lives at Kirton near Boston. The youngest son, Frederick, is a joiner and lives in Heighington. There are three grand children and eight great grand children.

And the celebrating couple had a quiet family re-union! In their later life they spent their summer holidays in Mablethorpe.

George and Betty Stiff on the dunes at Mablethorpe

What a sacrifice to send or allow five sons to go off to War, the family lost one son and two seriously injured. War Memorials throughout the county, and the country, show how family members were lost in such numbers.

George Stiff was Game keeper to Mr Herbert Dennis who was an enthusiastic sportsman. He not only shot pheasants and partridges with the syndicate, but he would have organised at least one Hare Shoot in a season.

Hare Shoot with 'Taffy' Dennis in the centre

This photo was taken before 1935 for it shows Taffy Dennis in the centre with his characteristic hat and a pipe in his mouth, with a group of people who are thought to be the beaters, as they are not carrying guns, or it may have been some local farmers. Anyway, they had had a good days shooting by the number of hares that had been caught. The work of the game keepers was an all year job - in the spring the broody hens sat upon the pheasant and partridge eggs to produce the little chicks, which had to be looked after until the summer when they were old enough to be released into the Woods. To keep the partridge stock healthy, eggs were swopped with the neighbouring estates of Sir David Hawley at Tumby and Lady Beryl Gilbert at Revesby and at one time some Hungarian eggs were imported to improve the vigour of the flock.

Then autumn preparing for "The Shooting Season" and winter Shooting.

Fred Sayer, 'Chick' Pask, Tom Stiff and Jean Stiff.

A Close up

Hen and Chicks

Tom Stiff – the Gamekeeper

From the other end of the Enclosure

The three Stiff girls Gwen, Jean and Ivy

Now onto the time that Tom Stiff was game keeper for the Estate. When his father retired, he moved from a cottage at Wasps Nest to one of the Gamekeepers' Cottages, in the Woods, with his wife and family of three daughters, Gwen, Ivy, and their youngest daughter, Jean, who still lives in the village and has kindly provided some of the photos for this chapter. Every gamekeeper had his dogs, here is Jean with Peter, a Black Labrador, and there are two others by their kennel. The lives of the Nocton gamekeepers are described in the following two articles. Tom retired in 1953, he and his wife moved into the village and lived in a cottage on Potterhanworth Road for nearly twenty years. Tom was the instigator of the Annual Clay Pigeon Shoot which raised money for the Cricket Club.

Jean with Peter the Black Retriever

Two other dogs

"The Good Old Days of Shooting" an article by Peter Scoley in one of the local papers in 1978, tells how he was one of the lucky people to take part in the old style shooting days. His great uncle was a member of the Nocton Estate shooting syndicate in the late 1950's, but he suffered from bad health and was unable to shoot on a regular basis, so he gave "his gun" to Peter who was only a lad of 20 years or so, which meant that he was the youngest member by 20 to 30 years. This allowed him to mix with men at the top of their professions who were paying large sums of money for their relaxation. They were some of the best shots in the United Kingdom, immaculate of manner in the shooting field, a requirement in any form of country pursuit. He remembers the light railway and compares it to a marvellous piece of superior Mecanno, and the trips down the Fen in the "Queen Mary". The train consisted of the engine, a coach for the guns - Queen Mary – from which the outfit took its name, a closed van for the beaters and loaders and an open truck at the back to carry the game. But Heath shoots were different, there an old game cart was used, drawn by a horse that had seen many winters, driven by Eustace Pask.

Eustace Pask with his horse and Game Cart

He was referred to as Old Pasky, for he had been doing this job for years and knew every trick in the book. It was his responsibility to see to the game, ensure that it was properly paired and hung on special racks in the cart. There was also another compartment in this vehicle over which he had special authority – the bar. The measures that he doled out were so large that the other guns made sure that Peter never had more than one. However, Old Pasky usually found an opportunity to "slive" round the leeward side of the cart and slip an illicit second drink, with a wink and a nod from his weather beaten old face. The highlight of the year was the "Big Wood Day", always followed by the annual dinner held at the Gamekeepers cottage. The main course was usually a full saddle of mutton, reputably wrapped in muslin and hung for two weeks from someone's apple tree. The meal was prepared by the Gamekeeper's wife and was always a culinary inspiration. Peter also wrote that the Gamekeeper (Tom Stiff) held more country lore in his little finger than most people learn in a lifetime.

The Game Cart went to an Oxford Museum in 1949.

There are two photos taken during the time that Mr John Ireson was Estate Manager. One shows him with four of the Guns – these are left to right Jack Francis, Bill Epton, John Ireson, Edward Horby and Ted Scoley, outside the passenger coach. The second one is a rest between drives.

Mr Ireson with his guests

Mr Ireson with fellow sportsmen taking a break December 12th 1953

Bob Jones wrote about shooting days on the Nocton Estate in the Summer 1988 edition of the "Insight" magazine. Without repeating too much, some of the previous points will be expanded. He wrote about the light railway, but explained that on Shoot Days, from

1927 until the mid 1950's a special train waited for "The Guns" at Nocton Station. There were two main rules to be observed. Firstly, you had to be at Nocton Station in time for the train's departure at 9 am sharp (if you missed, you had had it, as there were no hard roads down the fen) and secondly, shooting out of the train was forbidden. The coach for the guns was a splendid affair, some 20 feet long, with glass windows which wound down and was lined with oak panels. There were ten swivel seats each with a glass rack and legend is it that it was fitted out originally for the "Brass Hats" to tour the Western Front. It was so grand that it reminded some wag of the Royal Train and from then on it was known as the "Queen Mary". As it took nearly half an hour to reach the fen, a "snifter to clear your eye" was served. After the first drive, on re-entering the coach another drink was served "to keep the cold out". The Lincolnshire fens in winter can be very cold places with a chill factor that has to be experienced to be believed when standing waiting for the next drive to begin. The Nocton syndicate's practice of "having one to keep the cold out" at frequent intervals has proved so effective that no one has collapsed from hypothermia.

The generous hospitality was aided and abetted by a marvellous character called Eustace Pask, and the Captain of the syndicate stipulated that a measure to be "two fingers", but Pasky's problem was that not only did he have enormously thick gnarled fingers but, due to an accident years before, he had lost his middle finger. The resulting measure was two fingers separated by the missing one and thus filled the glass. The best pheasant shooting was in the 300 acre Big Wood with its immaculate rides cut like a golf course fairways and flanked on either side by great stands of rhododendron. There was in the Wood a large pit, this had provided the clay for the light railway to sit on, but it formed a kind of shooting bunker for the guns, who had to climb down wooden steps dug into its steep bank to reach their pegs. Pheasants rocketing over the high trees above it made for wonderful shooting to test the best shots of the day. On "wood" days the guns shot through to 3.30 pausing only for champagne and mince pies in one of the rides before making their way past the pollarded oaks, the Nine Brethren and the Seven Sisters, to the Keeper's Cottage where they partook of hotpot or a saddle of mutton. The guns vied with one another to produce the best bottle of port, and a Major Harry Greaves would arrive from Yorkshire with a Parkin cake which was alien to Lincolnshire tastes and a bottle of 1890 port that wasn't. At the end of the meal there would be Sweep on the day's bag, the proceeds of which were handed to Mrs Stiff for all her hard work.

The picture of "The Nine Brethren Tree" was taken during the winter of 1973. This remarkable tree has stood sentinel on the main drive through Nocton Wood for many centuries. It gets its name from its bole which is divided into nine separate trunks. As you can see, the trunks splay outwards, and several people can squeeze between them and stand up in the centre. The Oak is thought to have been one of the boundary markers between the Lord of the Manor's land and that belonging to the Priory, which once stood on Abbey Hill – a piece of rising ground overlooking Nocton Fen.

In the 1975 Particulars of Sale there is a small piece about the woods which says that "Nocton Big Wood is covered by the Forestry Commission's Dedication Scheme. The predominant species are oak together with ash, sycamore and birch with a little area to conifers. The present plan of operations for Big Wood ends in 1979.

But just before we leave the Big Wood we must mention "The Stage Coach" that lay abandoned in the woods during the 1960's.

The Old Stage Coach

Mrs Clark Richardson, who was born at Wasps Nest, recollected in July 1984 that the Stage Coach was owned by Squire John Hodgson and was used to transport passengers and guests to and from the Nocton and Dunston Station or to Town (presumably Lincoln). It was painted a light brown khaki colour with gold trimmings. Two men in khaki green livery and wearing brown top hats rode on top of the coach, one with a horn, he was responsible for opening gates and the doors of the coach while the other was in charge of the four horses. The luggage also travelled on top. She was a school girl at Nocton School at this time, which was about 1900, she remembered that the coach had six or seven windows.

Mr Field from Washingborough did a lot of research about the Stage Coach that he found in a derelict state in the woods, and he made a scale model. He found out that it was a Horse-drawn Bus of a type used in the Manchester Area, and there was no records of it being used on routes in Lincoln. It was believed to have been brought from Bradford where John Hodgson had many interests. The Horse Bus was introduced to Manchester in 1825 by John Greenway, by 1865 his Manchester Carriage Company Ltd was running 90 vehicles. Then the trams were introduced and by

1901 the company owned 515 trams and only 26 Horse drawn Buses. There is only one of the original buses in good condition left and this is in the Transport Museum in Manchester. A small amount of paint was found on the poor old coach, this was deep red up to the windows and cream above, these were the colours of the Manchester Carriage Company. Motor vehicles were introduced in the 1920's and this stage coach was made redundant and it eventually ended up in the woods being used by the gamekeepers, for there was a small stove in one corner when it was found. The Horse drawn coach was believed to have been taken to Doddington Hall for renovation.

There is a table of the previous three shooting seasons included in the particulars. (Table of Game Birds shot in 1922 to1925).

SPORTING.					
The Estate is reputed to be one of the best sporting properties in the County, and in an average season with fair keepering and rearing should yield a bag of approximately as given for the past three years :—					
			1922/23.	1923/24.	1924/25.
Pheasants ..	..	..	3,229	3,029	3,165
Partridges ..	..	..	1,481	1,736	1,344
Hares	..	..	832	1,212	749
Wild Duck	..	..	103	183	9
Woodcock ..	..	..	26	32	25
Rabbits	..	..	2,739	1,875	2,843
Snipe	..	..	5	14	22
Various	..	..	32	49	47
Note.—The above bag includes about 700 acres of rented Shooting.					

SEASON	Pheasants	Partridges	Hares	Snipe	Woodcock	Wild Duck
1969/70	5,542	727	499	4	42	205
1970/71	7,163	1,063	764	2	51	9
1971/72	4,427	737	584	2	27	67
1972/73	4,080	435	1,379	2	33	49
1973/74	4,741	640	949	2	27	76
1974/75	4,082	531	422	1	39	3

(List of the Game Bags for 1969 – 1975).

Recycling

CHAPTER 13
Onto Abbey Hill, Wasps Nest and the Fen

Leaving the Big Wood, we come out onto a plateau. To your left is an area known as Abbey Hill. For it was here that a Priory for Black Canons of the Order of St. Augustine was founded by Robert d'Arcy in the time of King Stephen. Robert's father had crossed to England with William the Conqueror in 1066 and the family owned a lot of land in Lincolnshire, which included the manors or estates of Nocton and Dunston. The members of the family acted as patrons of and benefactors to the Priory, but at that time the village churches had been given to the Benedictine Abbey of St. Mary in York. But sometime in the late twelfth century both churches were presented to the Prior and Canons of Nocton Park by Thomas d'Arcy, the founder's grandson or great-grandson, this of course created some problems. The agricultural economy throughout the life of the Priory was based on mixed farming.

Lincolnshire Longwool sheep.

Seal of Nocton Park Priory

Sheep played an important role in the earlier Middle Ages, with the Priory exporting some 500 fleeces annually by 1300. At this time, the Wool Trade was at its height, with Lincolnshire fleeces being rated the third best in the country and a fleece from the area south of Lincoln was highly sought after. Boston was the third most important port in the country, and there are records of sacks of wool being delivered to Boston from as far away as Coventry. This wool was bought by Continental bankers / merchants and was exported to Flanders, Italy and France. In 1534 by the Act of Supremacy, Henry VIII declared himself to be the supreme head of the Church of England. Thomas Hornell, prior of Nocton Park Priory, the sub-dean John Trwe, and two canons had no choice but to sign the Acknowledgement of the Royal Supremacy, and in effect this sounded the death knell of the Priory. This is the Seal of the Priory attached to the document, dated 30 July 1534 which is still in the Public Record

Office. It represents the Prior kneeling to the right before St. Mary Magdalene, crowned in a garden. In March 1536, it was declared by Parliament that all religious houses with less than twelve monks or nuns and less than £200 a year income should be closed down. Nocton Park Priory fell into this category on both counts for their income was only £60 six shillings and a half penny. The leaving date was 29th September, Prior Hornell was granted a pension of ten marks by the Crown and later became vicar of Metheringham, his canons each received twenty shillings. In 1537, the house and land was leased by the Crown for twenty one years to Thomas Wymbyshe then Lord of the Manor of Nocton. But the following year Henry VIII gave the site and the lease to his brother-in-law, Charles Brandon, Duke of Suffolk. In 1569, the Priory site was granted to Sir Henry Stanley, Lord Strange on the forfeiture of the Duke of Suffolk's family lands to Queen Elizabeth, and he had a private house built on the site of the Priory. However, it was pulled down about a 100 years later, and by about 1690 Sir William Ellys had built the first Nocton Hall in the same area as the ruined third Nocton Hall now stands. There are no remains of the Priory to be seen above the ground - Mr Edward Howard remembered the Priory Well being filled in the 1860's by a Charles Toynbee - but broken hillocks and uneven ground still mark the site. And it was here that the ashes of Herbert Dennis were scattered to the four winds as described in an earlier chapter.

Sheep are a focal point once again. For the large field on your right was set to pasture and was used for the Sheep Dog Trials for many years. David and Gill Rumbelow came to Nocton in 1971, when David took

David Rumbelow in 1983 with his three Border Collies, Glen, Bonnie and Mist.

Shepherds and farmers from all over the country competed in the trials. The trials were well attended by the local community and from the wider community and the attendance numbers ran into the hundreds. The whole of the village community were involved running a refreshment tent, produce stall, tombola, raffle, and traditional games like skittles. There were tractor and trailer rides for the children and tours of the estate for the grown-ups. The Village Social Club manned a bar. At the end of the day, all the Cups and the raffle prizes were presented by the Estate manager's wife."

On the tenth anniversary, in July 1983, a reporter interviewed David for an article in the local press and this is what he said. "We expect about 300 people will turn up to see more than 30 competitors with 58 dogs from Wales, Leicestershire, Yorkshire and Lancashire as well as Lincolnshire." Among them will be Jim Dyson, David's close friend from Llangollen, the 1981 international shepherd champion. He will find that, unlike some other trials, Nocton will provide fresh sheep for each competitor to run. "We plan to use 300 of Nocton Farms' flock of 1200 Suffolk cross," he explains. "They are a good heavy sheep which will take a bit more pushing around the course than the hill sheep used at 'other trials'." In addition to shepherds and farmers, the entry comprises a few contestants described by David as 'Businessmen.' He said: "You can pay £1,500 or £1,700 for a good dog these days and the world of sheepdog trials attracts a number of people who can buy their way in." But no-one will lift big prizes at Nocton where the top money on offer is £25.

up the position of Shepherd for Nocton Farms Ltd. He had previously worked for the Marquis of Exeter at Burghley House, at Stamford. After eighteen months in his new job, he became involved with the setting up the Nocton Sheep Dog Trials that brought two notable benefits to the Village.

David has been kind enough to write this piece for the book, which explains a little more about the Sheep Dog Trials and the fund raising aspect of the Day.

"The first Nocton Sheep Dog Trial was in 1973 and continued for over 20 years. I was the shepherd for Nocton Farms Ltd having an interest in and competing in Sheep Dog Trials, I saw an opportunity to raise money for Nocton Village Hall and for the various clubs that used the Village Hall, to also raise funds for their clubs. The Village Clubs in the early 1970's included a Tufty Club for children to learn about Road Safety which was run by Mrs Phil Sands, the Women's Institute, the Friendship Club for people aged over sixty, the Social Club and the Youth Club.

Jim Smart, the Director of Nocton Farms Ltd, which incidentally had previously during his directorship been owned by Smith Potato Estates, was enthusiastic and supportive of the idea. The farm provided the field and the man power to set the scene with tents and other amenities. Companies that supported Nocton Farms Ltd were generous in their sponsorship, both cash donations and prizes. (Townsends, J.A. Andrews & Son, Chris Howard, Orchard House Vet Surgery, just to mention a few).

21st Anniversary of Nocton Sheep Dog Trials July 17th 1994.

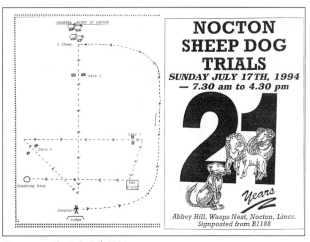

Programme for July 17th 1994.

OFFICIALS		
Judge	:	Mr. Murdoch
Timekeeper	:	Mr. John Kissane Bardney, Lincoln
Commentator	:	Mr. David Rumbelow Nocton, Lincoln
Course Director	:	Mr. David Rumbelow Nocton, Lincoln
Secretary	:	Mrs. Doreen Green Nocton, Lincoln

SINGLE DOG - CLASS 1 OPEN

1st Prize	:	SMITHS POTATO ESTATES PERPETUAL CHALLENGE CUP, TANKARD AND £50.
2nd Prize	:	£25, 3rd £20, 4th £15, 5th £10, 6th £5, 7th £3, 8th £2.

CLASS 2 NOVICE

1st Prize	:	COOPERS ANIMAL HEALTH PERPETUAL NOVICE TROPHY AND WILES FERTILISERS PERPETUAL CHALLENGE SILVER TRAY and £10.
2nd Prize	:	£5, 3rd £3.

DOUBLES

1st Prize	:	WELLCOME FOUNDATION PERPETUAL CHALLENGE CUP and £10.
2nd Prize	:	£5, 3rd £3.

The Committee would like to thank all those people involved in the running of the trials and stands.

The Committee would like to thank the following Companies and Individuals who have supported the trials with cash donations or prizes.

J. A. Andrews & Son
B & M Services
Boston Tractors
Branston Packers plc
British Field Products Limited
Brown & Co
Brown Butlin Limited
Chandlers (Farm Equipment) Ltd
Dalgety Agriculture Limited
W. Everard & Son
Farm Electronics
Hodgson Elkington & Co
Stored Crop Conservation Ltd
L. W. Housham Ltd.
Chris Howard
Jacksons Laundry
Javelin Water Engineering Ltd.
R. Larrington Trailers
Newlin Oil Co Ltd
Orchard House Vet Surgery
Blankney Estates Ltd
McKinnells
Mr. Tonge
Sharpes International Seeds
A. L. Shaw & Son Ltd
F. Townsend & Son Ltd
TRP Limited
Central Wool Growers Ltd
Walkers Smiths Snack Foods Ltd
Salveson Food Services
Odling Bros.

The facilities and the sheep have been placed at our disposal by Nocton Farms Limited.

David was the shepherd on the estate for 27 years until he was made redundant in 1999.

David and Gill have brought up two sons, the eldest, Gareth now lives in Australia with his family, while Ian lives locally with his wife and two young daughters.

David has played his part in the running of the Village, for he has held positions on lots of Committees and at the present time is a Councillor of the Nocton Parish Council and serves on the Nocton Village Hall Management Committee

Heading north, we descend down to Wasps Nest looking out across "The Fen" towards the River Witham and to Bardney.

View of the Fens with Wasps Nest houses on the left.

Abbey Hill Cottages described in the 1891 Census, but taken later with new council houses behind.

There were a large number of people living in this area, in the 1890's. The vicar held regular meetings in the large farmhouses on the Fen. The Howards from Nocton Rise had a Fen Farm as well as the Wrights from the Heath.

Extract from Church Magazines 1898
"Thursday 6th January – A large and encouraging congregation met at Mr Drage's house on Mr Howard's Bottom Fen Farm at 7pm. The interest in these Fen gatherings seemed to decline during the summer, but it has revived again since the long evenings set in. The Vicar's expositions of Scripture have a great attraction for the dwellers of our Fen".

From the 1891 Census, we find that there were two cottages standing here, referred to as Abbey Hill Cottages. Harry Gilbert lived in one with his wife, Sarah and their two children – Lucy who was eleven and born in Greetham (just east of Horncastle) and Amos who was five and born in the parish of Nocton. Next door lived the Clayton family. Joseph, who was a Paralytic, his wife, Charlotte, and their three young children, also his elder brother Samuel, they were all born in Nocton parish except for Charlotte who came from Branston.

This Census goes on to record that there were another 21 inhabited dwellings on the Fens with 145 persons living in them, of which sixty one were adults, twenty four were aged between 12 and 17, while there were sixty children aged eleven and under. Only two Head of Household were referred to as "Farmer", William Gray, who was born at Boston, and William Booth from Timberland. Most of the inhabitants were born in Lincolnshire, from Gainsborough in the West, Boston in the East to Market Deeping in the South and everywhere in between. The Agricultural Foremen were the people who moved around most, for William Compton was born at Revesby whilst his wife came from Blankney, four of their children were born at Revesby, three at Blankney and they must have moved to Nocton about 1890 for their one year old was born here. There were three young Farm Servants living in the Fens at this time, Herbert Asher, 16, from Burton Pedwardine, Richard Foster, 18, from Lowdham Nottinghamshire, and Horace Moss, 18, from some unknown town in Kent. There was a widow visiting from Barrow on Humber and staying in one of the houses with her two young children. Only two dwellings are mentioned by name, one the Engine House and the other was Decoy Farm. Frederick Cordey was the Engine Driver and he lived with his wife and 15 year old grand daughter. He left within the next ten years for in the 1901 census a William Kent from Fiskerton and his wife, Ada, from Skellingthorpe, had taken up residence. While William Rickell from Crowthorn in Yorkshire, described as an Agricultural Foreman, lived at Decoy Farm, with his wife, Susannah and their five children and two Farm Servants, aged 17 and 20, and a twelve year old Domestic Servant. The family had moved around for their eldest child was born at Normanby by Spital, and the others at Farthorpe, Sandy Park in Nottinghamshire, Dunston and Nocton. They moved again within a few years, for in the 1901 Census Tom Sewell had moved to the Decoy Farm.

Decoy Farm house

Tom was listed as a "Farmer" and had been born in Bloxholme while his wife Sarah came from Navenby. They had not moved very far for their eight children were born either in Waddington or Metheringham. Also residing with them were two servants, twelve people in one house.

The Recording Officer, David Bratt, the Schoolmaster would have set off down the Fen visiting the dwellings on the Southside of the road until he reached the River Witham and the Engine House and returned visiting the houses on the Northside. The last house to visit was the farm on the left hand side at Wasps Nest.

Edenbrow's Farmhouse, taken in early 1900's with the Car Dyke on your right.

Why is it called Wasps Nest? There are many theories, one that it was a pub name and this one amongst others, which sounds more realistic. A very old woman by the name of Granny Clayton lived down Nocton Fen and she used to tell many strange stories, according to her, the original Wasps Nest was a building which had an outer door from every room to the yard – like the cells of a wasps nest, and that it was a haunt of highwaymen, who would have an easy escape route. A priest's hole was also found in the chimney of the building, which would also have given the highwaymen a hiding place.

It was here the Edenbrows lived. Poucher Edenbrow, who was born in Dorrington in 1855, his wife, Susanna, who was a year younger and originated from North Hykeham (when it was a village and not a dormitory town). In the 1891 Census, they had six children attending school, the eldest was William who was 13, and two toddlers at home, they were all born in the parish of Nocton, and little Alice was born four years later. These photos were take in the early 1900's, showing the family outside their Back Door, Harvesting with the Reaper and then Threshing

Another Extract from the Church Magazine, November 1899.

"There was a record attendance of more than a hundred worshippers at Mr Edenbrow's house on the evening of Thursday, the 5th October, when the Nocton

Edenbrow Family outside their back door.

Threshing

Fen Bible reading Service was devoted to rendering 'Thanks to Giver of the Harvest'. The house had been decorated by the Edenbrow family, assisted by Mrs Gilbert, Miss Dykes and Miss F Denton. The whole heartedness which marks all such gatherings in the Fen was very evident throughout the proceedings. The Vicar gave addresses upon the 147th Psalm and the 15th chapter of St. Matthew; and the hymns included "We plough the fields and scatter", "Have you heard the glad new song?" and the "Old Hundredth". Mr Kenneth Dykes conducted the sale at the close of the service and the proceed together with the collections amounted to £4 11s".

One of Poucher Edenbrow's grand daughters, Phil Sands, wrote this in 2004 about her grand parents. Poucher Edenbrow married Susannah Collishaw at Kirby Green in 1874. Poucher worked for Robert Wright, farmer at Nocton Heath, who bought the Fen Farm in 1877 and placed Poucher as the manager. This was a dairy farm plus breeders of Lincoln Red cattle and Long wool Sheep, which were sent off to the Argentine. Susannah made and sold butter, proceeds given to Robert Wright each week. Poucher was paid ten shillings per week and the men eight shillings. Poucher and Susannah had 12 children, Annie, John, William, Thomas, Lucy, Mary, Edith, Fredrick, Harriet, Susannah, Ethel and Alice. Ethel worked as nanny to Squire Hodgson's children at Nocton Hall, and Embsay House in the early 1910's, and also to Mr and Mrs Charles Howard's children at Nocton Rise. Ethel married Clark Richardson in 1912 and lived and farmed at Cottage Farm, Dunston.

Ethel and Alice

Cutting the harvest with the Reaper.

But some twelve years earlier, Annie married Thomas Atkin on 31st July 1900, both were aged 24. The ceremony was held in Nocton Church, officiated by the Rev. Footman. A photo was taken in "A Cabbage Patch" showing the Groom and Bride, with her brother, William, sister Lucy and cousin Jessie Atkin and father Poucher Edenbrow.

Annie's Wedding Photograph taken in a Cabbage Patch.

Lucy and Alice were taught dressmaking by Miss Semper who lived in the Old Row in the village, and would have used their bicycles to make the journey to the village. In the 1901 census, many of the women living in the village were described as dressmakers. The Boys of the Edenbrow family worked on the farm

Susannah and Ethel with their bicycles.

Tom, Jack (John), Poucher and William Edenbrow.

Picture of fen workers with their hoes – Mrs Howard, Mr Richardson, Mrs Birkett, Mrs Pullen, Mrs Harrison, Mr Baldock, Mrs Pilsworth, Miss Trafford, Mrs Elvin, Mrs Drage, and Miss Richardson.

Extract from the Church Newsletter dated May 1912 *"On February 27, instead of the usual service in the Fen, the Vicar gave a lecture, illustrated by lantern views on "Peary's Dash for the North Pole". The gathering was a very large one and was held at Mrs. Woods' House (Mill Drain Farm), and Mr. G. H. Woods presided".*

There was a lot of activity during the time that the Dennises owned the Estate. The laying of the light railway allowed the Fen community easier access to the village, this was mentioned earlier in the book. There were still many farmsteads and houses at this time, but the land had been taken "In Hand", so the Heath farmers ceased to farm on the fen, and it was all managed by Major Webber. It was about 1946,

when Smiths Potato Estates employed Mr Ireson as Estate Manager that a "Village Hall" was erected at Wasps Nest for the use of the people who lived down on the fen. A Nocton Fen Social Club was formed, and a report in the S.P.C Magazine dated October 1949, describes an Annual Garden Party on the 9th July which was opened by the Manager's wife, Mrs Ireson. She was presented with a bouquet of flowers and an enjoyable evening was had by all with a profit of £31 declared. The following month, the Sunday School children held their annual Tea Party and Sports, under the supervision of the Vicar, Miss Redshaw, and Mr Sands. A very enjoyable time was spent at the end of which, each child took home a bottle of pop and a bag of Smiths Crisps.

A gathering of the Fen Folk outside the recently erected Fen Village Hall about 1948.

Miss Jean Redshaw on 6th July 1949.

Mrs Ireson was keen to introduce activities for the women, for she formed WI groups in both Nocton and Dunston as well as one in Nocton Fen.

1955 – Wasps Nest Ladies Group at RAF Nocton Hall

1956 – Wasps Nest Ladies Group in the grounds of RAF Nocton Hall.

We have two photos, from the mid 1950's, of ladies with some Airmen from RAF Nocton Hall having a photo call in the grounds of Nocton Hall with Mrs Ireson in both and Mr Ireson seated with some children in one of them. The caption with them reads "Wasps Nest Ladies Group".

Partridge Farm showing the corn stacks.

In the 1950's, the cottages and houses in the fen were without electricity and mains water, and it became an estate policy not to modernise these properties, but to spend money on the cottages in Nocton and Dunston villages, which did not have indoor toilets and bathrooms, as mentioned in the section about Wellhead Lane. The employees and their families from the fens gradually moved up to the villages leaving the cottages empty. These houses were all taken down in the late 1960's, with a record that Decoy House was pulled down in 1968, and all that now remains are a few agricultural sheds and a "Beet Pad" or two. But it was in 1958 that the Nocton Fen Village Hall was closed owing to the reduced number of people living

in the fens. The only houses allowed to remain were in reasonably good condition standing near the top of the fen at Wasps Nest. It was here many years earlier, that Tom Stiff and his family lived in one of these brick built houses. So the tradition was continued when Sam Clark came in the late 1960's, to be Game keeper for the Nocton Estate. By 1993, Sam and his son looked after one of the best known shoots in the area. He provided twenty days' shooting a

Sam Clark, gamekeeper in the 1990s

year for the Estate, plus a few for a syndicate that paid a handsome annual subscription for the privilege. On Shoot days, Sam's duties included finding up to forty beaters, and marshalling them here and there to their required positions, picking up the game and organising the lunchtime refreshments etc. Part of their duties included controlling predators such as weasels, crows and grey squirrels, as well as rearing and feeding the pheasants. In many respects Sam and many others like him, see themselves as wardens of the countryside, knowing a great deal about the plants, animals and their habitats. Sam has recently retired and his son has taken over his father's position.

Len Woodhead was born, brought up and worked on the Nocton Fen and has written a book about his life. "A Lincolnshire Lad Looks Back".

Now we are ready to return to the Village, leaving behind a large acreage of land with only a handful of people living at the area we call Wasps Nest. The Abbey Hill Cottages and the two pairs of council houses have been owner occupied for about twenty years.

CHAPTER 14
Returning to the Village

We will return to the village by way of the Bottom Lodge. This was built in the times when the Lord of the Manor liked to impress his visitors who passed by on their way to the Hall, for this house had ten chimney stacks and only one fireplace. It was here that Eustace Pask was born in 1876, the family soon moved to live in the village at the Ten Row. The 1891 census only mentions two Lodges, one was referred to as "Hall Lodge" and was near Manor Farm on Potterhanworth Road, and the other "Nocton Hall Lodge" and this one was near the uninhabited Gamekeepers Cottage, followed by Nocton Heath. So we do not know who was living in the Bottom Lodge in 1891, later it was used by agricultural workers on the Smiths Potato Estates and later Nocton Farms, and following a fire in the mid 1990's it has been rebuilt and is now occasionally occupied.

Next door is the Cricket Ground. Cricket has been played in the village for a long time. An extract from the Parish Magazine of March 1907 explains that cricket has been played on this field for a great many years.

Much of this information has been gleaned from the Church Magazines that have been produced over the years. The extract opposite is from the February 1880 Church Magazine and shows the List of Subscribers and the Statement of Accounts for 1879 Season.

This extract from the August 1898 Nocton Church Magazine talks about a
"Testimonial to Mr. Roberts" – 'Our old friend and fellow-parishioner, Mr William Roberts, was presented on the 20th July, with a beautiful and valuable testimonial, consisting of a richly embossed salad bowl of Wedgewood Ware with silver servers, a silver mustard-pot, two silver pepper-boxes, and four silver salt-cellars and spoons. About forty subscribers, including the Marquis of Ripon and Mr John Hodgson, contributed to the gift to mark their appreciation of the long and valuable services rendered by Mr Roberts to the Nocton Cricket Club. All are agreed in recognising the good judgement, firmness and fairness which Mr Roberts displayed as captain and as umpire; while the open handed hospitality with which he always entertained friends and opponents will ever be one of the pleasantest recollections of the Nocton Cricket Club'.

We print below the accounts of the Nocton Cricket Club. We are delighted that its financial state is not less prosperous than its professional career has been:—

List of Subscriptions for Season 1879.

	£	s.	d.		£	s.	d.
The Marquis of Ripon	2	2	0	Messrs. C. Greenfield &			
The Earl de Grey	1	1	0	Paddison	0	10	0
Rev. A. C. Wilson	1	1	0	„ Cleaver & Cartler	0	10	0
Mrs. Wilson	0	10	6	„ E. J. Howard & D. Bratt	0	10	0
Mr. Stirling	0	10	6	„ W. Fox & S. Noble	0	10	0
Mr. Herford	0	10	6	„ Bacon & Ripley	0	10	0
Mr. Evans	0	10	6	„ Copping & Grebby	0	10	0
Mr. Glyn	0	10	6	„ Headland & Hicks	0	10	0
Mr. R. A. Thorpe	0	10	6	„ Melbourne & Grantham	0	10	0
Mr. J. A. Thorpe	0	10	6	To Balance brought forward			
Mr. Papillon	0	7	6	from 1878	0	8	5
Messrs. Jackson & Armitead	0	10	0	To Cash from the Nocton			
„ R. Wright & W. Wright	0	10	0	Sports Committee	5	12	0
„ W. Roberts & J. Roberts	0	10	0				
„ C. Roberts & M. Roberts	0	10	0		£20	15	5
„ F. Battle & Ridsdale	0	10	0				

Statement of Accounts for Season 1879.

Cr.	£	s.	d.	Dr.	£	s.	d.
To Total Amount of Sub-				By Ground Expenses	0	19	0
scriptions 1879	20	15	5	„ Expenses at Matches	2	3	0
				„ Stationery	0	5	0
				„ Noble's Bill for Box and			
				Work	2	1	6
				„ Gale's bill for Balls, Gloves,			
To Amount	20	15	5	Bats, Stumps, &c.	5	8	10
By Amount	10	17	4		£10	17	4
To Balance	£9	18	1				

Audited 23rd March, 1880. W. ROBERTS, Chairman,
R. A. THORPE, Secretary.

SEASON 1880.

Patrons—The Marquis of Ripon, K.G. | President and Treasurer—
Earl de Grey. | Rev. A. C. Wilson.

Committee—Messrs. Bratt, Evans, C. Greenfield, Howard, Hilton, Lissington, Ridsdale, Roberts, R. Thorpe, J. Thorpe, R. Wright, W. Wright, and Rev. E. H. Morgan.

Officers—Mr. W. Roberts, Captain.
R. A. Thorpe, Secretary and Vice-Captain.

1879 List of Subscribers

According to the 1891 Census, a William Roberts lived in or near the centre of the village and was described as a Farmer who had been born in Ragnall in Nottinghamshire.

There appears to have been a period when there was no cricket club in the village, for in 1907 at a Young Men's Club meeting in February there was a discussion to form a cricket club and by March the Parish Magazine reports that 'We are glad to hear that the Cricket Club is taking definite shape. The field known as "The Thoroughfare Close", part of the Glebe Land, was formerly used for cricket, and by arrangement between Mr. W. Wray, Mr. W. Fish and the Vicar, this field is again available for the purposes of the new club. We hope the parishioners will shew a practical interest in this new and excellent scheme. We understand that Cricketers from Dunston and

Potterhanworth are eligible for membership in the new club'.

Another report in the July 1908 Church Magazine tells about a Cricket Match in which Nocton played a team from Thornton near Bradford. (Mr George Hodgson came from Thornton Mills, near Bradford). It was on 8th June that the visiting team came and won the match and were later entertained along with the villagers at the Whit Monday Garden Party, in the Vicarage gardens. We may note that the Thornton team were entertained to lunch in the club room, at the expense of Mr. N. Hodgson, and they formally expressed their thanks to him, and also to the Vicar for hospitality during the day. After the visitors left to return home, we presume by train, the local team played a "Broomstick Cricket Match". A very amusing match played between the young men and the young girls, with the young men using broomsticks and left handed while the girls played right handed. Needless to say the young men won.

An extract from the May 1921 Nocton Parish Magazine prints the fixtures of the Cricket Club for June:- June 1st, v. Cranwell; 11th, v. Digby; 18th, v. Blankney; July 2nd, v. Bardney. An effort is being made to make these events an opportunity for spending a pleasant afternoon, and with this in view tea will be served on the ground on Saturdays at a nominal charge of 6d. Those who can afford to contribute to the tea fund are asked to do so, and any member of the club will be happy to receive contributions of any amount.

Cricket Team 1930's before WWII

This photo shows the Cricket Team taken in the 1930's before the WWII. Bernard Plumtree is sitting in the centre of the front row, he signed up and went off to the War and was one of the unfortunate villagers not to return home. The team are named as (back row) T.Stiff, J.Day, G.Denton, W.Redshaw, Capt Roberson, C.Brown, C.Bosworth, and F.Eminson and the front row - H.Allgood, G.Cornwall, B.Plumtree, G.Ianson, and M.Young.

This photo could have been taken on the same day, showing the team in action.

Cricket Match about 1930's

An extract from the September 1939 Parish Magazine states "Once again the Cricket Club is indebted to Mr.C.T.Stiff for a most excellent Clay Pigeon Shoot. It was held on Saturday, July 29th, and brought competitors from far and near, and as one of them remarked, there was finer shooting than he had ever seen. The gift of a challenge cup by Mr F. Smith added considerably to the keenness of the Competition. This was won by Mr. A.Gray from Saxilby. Mr Goode of Grantham, acted as the judge, and the vicar, on behalf of Mr C.F Young, presented the prizes, which took place when darkness was fast falling". (It is amazing how people travelled about in those days).

On the following page are the 1947 and 1948 Programmes with the Officials and Committee also the Fixture List for the year.

An extract from The S.P.C.Magazine dated October 1949, reports 'The season has drawn to a close, we take stock of the progress and achievements made.

Out of a total of 33 matches played, 17 have been won and 15 lost, which is quite satisfactory when it is realised that the whole 40 playing members have been given games. Outstanding in the averages both with the bat and ball is Norman "Digger" Harvey. He has scored 284 runs in 20 innings, being three times not out for an average of 16.7, and with the ball has taken 73 wickets at a rate of 4.7 runs each. Other notable performers with the bat are :- A.Bee 185 runs, av.14.2, E Pask 141 runs, av. 9.2, G Parkinson 107 runs, av. 8.9 and Bob Pask 137 runs, av.8.5, and with the ball :- Fred Wilford 30 wickets, av. 4.7, C.Bryan 39 wickets, av.6.4, E Pask 35 wickets, av. 8.8.

On the 20th August, a representative eleven attended the wedding of Norman Harvey to Miss Olive King, at Metheringham, and formed an archway of bats and wickets through which the happy couple emerged when leaving the church. The team afterwards attended the reception. Best wishes were offered to Norman and Olive for a long and happy married life'.

NOCTON CRICKET CLUB

SEASON 1947

President : F. SMITH, Esq.

Vice-Presidents :

Cyril J. Scott, Esq.   Sir Herbert E. Morgan, k.b.e.
F. Le-Neve Foster, Esq.   G. F. Young, Esq.
W. R. Roberson, Esq.   J. Ireson, Esq.
C. F. Eminson, Esq.   Mrs. Ireson
Mrs. Kennington   E. M. Howard, Esq.
J. H. Greaves, Esq.   Ald. G. Flintham
Rev. K. Healey   W. Smalley, Esq.
E. R. Semper, Esq.

Chairman: J. Ireson, Esq.

Vice-Chairman: W. R. Roberson, Esq.

Captain: C. Bryan.   *Vice-Captain:* H. Carratt.

Hon. Sec: A. Eadie.   *Asst. Hon. Sec.:* E. Turner.

Hon. Treasurer: C. Bryan.

Committee:

D. Turner, T. Stiff, A. Melton, H. Redshaw, F. Redshaw,
H. Jackson, W. Jackson, A. T. Day, E. Redshaw,
M. Reek, F. Willford, R. Pask, E. Pask, C. Yates, C. White

SUBSCRIPTION : Adults, 4/- ; Youths under 17 years, 2/6.

KEYWORTH & SONS, SWANPOOL COURT, LINCOLN

1947 Programme

NOCTON *versus:—*					
May 17th.	L.N.E.R.	..	..	..	Home
„ 24th.	Branston	..	..	..	Away
„ 31st.	Martin ..	..	..	..	Home
June 7th.	Billinghay	..	..	..	Home
„ 14th.	Skellingthorpe		..	..	Home
„ 28th.	Heighington	..		..	Away
July 5th.	L.N.E.R.	..	..	..	Home
„ 12th.	Martin ..	..	..	..	Away
„ 19th.					
„ 26th.					
Aug. 2nd.			..	..	
„ 9th.	Billinghay	..	..	..	Away
„ 16th.	Heighington	..	..	..	Home
„ 23rd.	Skellingthorpe		..	..	Away
„ 30th.	Digby ..	..	..	..	Away

Evening Matches as arranged.

Practice Nights :
TUESDAY and THURSDAY.

1947 Programme

NOCTON CRICKET CLUB

SEASON 1948

President: F. SMITH, Esq.

Vice-Presidents:

Cyril J. Scott, Esq.   Sir Herbert E. Morgan, k.b.e.
F. Le-Neve Foster, Esq.   G. F. Young, Esq.
C. F. Eminson, Esq.   J. Ireson, Esq.
Admiral Lambert, d.s.o.   Mrs. Ireson
J. H. Greaves, Esq.   E. M. Howard, Esq.
Rev. K. Healey   Rev. A. R. Hall, b.a.
E. R. Semper, Esq.   Ald. G. Flintham
A. Francis, Esq.   H. H. Leven, Esq.

Chairman: J. Ireson, Esq.

Vice-Chairman: T. Stiff, Esq.

Captain: C. Bryan.   *Vice-Captain:* E. Pask.

Hon. Sec.: A. Eadie.   *Asst. Hon. Sec.:* E. Turner.

Hon. Treasurer: C. Bryan.

Committee:

D. Turner, A. Melton, H. Redshaw, A. Bee, F. Redshaw,
H. Jackson, E. Redshaw, C. Yates, M. Reek, R. Pask,
H. Carratt.

SUBSCRIPTION : Adults, 4/- ; Youths under 17 years, 2/6.

KEYWORTH & SONS, SWANPOOL COURT, LINCOLN.

1948 Programme

NOCTON *versus:—*					
May 1st.	Robeys	..	..	..	Home
„ 8th.	Ruskington	..	..	..	Away
„ 15th.	Potterhanworth ..		..	..	Home
„ 17th.	Branston ..	..	..		Away
„ 22nd.	Robeys	..	..	..	Away
„ 29th.	Kirkby Green	..	..	..	Home
June 5th.	Billinghay	..	..	..	Home
„ 12th.	Heighington	..	..	..	Home
„ 19th.	Nocton R.A.F.	..	..	..	Away
„ 26th.	Ruskington	..	..	..	Home
July 3rd.	Kirkby Green	..	..	..	Away
„ 10th.	Nocton R.A.F.	..	..	..	Home
„ 17th.	Digby ..	..	..	..	Away
„ 24th.	Potterhanworth ..		..	..	Away
„ 31st.	Billinghay ..	..	..	..	Away
Aug. 2nd.	Branston ..	..	..	..	Home
„ 7th.	Washingborough	..	..	..	Home
„ 14th.	Heighington	..	..	..	Away
„ 21st.	Digby ..	..	..	..	Home
„ 28th.	Washingborough	..	..	..	Away

Evening Matches as arranged.

Practice Nights :—
TUESDAY and THURSDAY.

1948 Programme

Cricket Team 1956

We move on to 1956 for this picture.
Back row:- Umpire not known, A Bee, R Redshaw, Mrs T Asher, N Harvey, Hendry, and R Pask. Front row - Don Turner, F Willford, C Bryan, John Ireson (Estate Manager for Smiths Potato Estate), E Pask, Ray Lowin, and D Creasey.

Don Turner told many a story about establishing the level cricket pitch that we know today. As many of you will know, the field is ridge and furrowed, either medieval strip farming or more likely Victorian furrows because of the straight ends. The estate workers used to take the spare soil from the riddled potatoes and from the elevators lifting the sugar beet and take this to the cricket pitch to help to make it level. Don also said that the teams used to play on Wednesday afternoons, whether that was for practices or for matches it is not clear. Tony Jackson played for the team in the early 1960's.

Tony Jackson about 1960

The cricket club was disbanded in 1980 but was reformed in 1989, with friendly matches inside the village eg Nocton Farms -v- The Village.

Photo call for the Opening Match 1990

The following year the opening friendly match was on 29th July 1990 against Blankney. Back row - Ben Clapton, Peter Cooke, Chris Hubbard, Paul Turner, David Hardy, David Franklin, Alistair Grant, and Peter Franklin. Front row - John Watt, John Clapton (Secretary), David Glew (Captain for the day), Philip Franklin (Chairman), and Ian Green. The appointed Captain, Robin Hubbard, was unable to play on this particular day.

Cricket Team 1991

A photo of the Nocton Cricket Club taken on the 4th May 1991 just before the match against the George and Dragon. This was their first home league match in the first season of the membership of the Lincoln & District Cricket League playing in Division 4. Back row - David Franklin, Neil Faulkner, Alistair Grant, Paul Chambers, Ben Clapton, Peter Cooke, Ian Green and Paul Turner. Front row - David Glew, John Clapton, Robin Hubbard (Captain), Peter Franklin, and Philip Franklin.

It was in February 1994, that the members of Nocton Cricket Club were delighted to be reunited with their old pavilion. Heighington Cricket Club had bought the building when Nocton Cricket Club closed down. They had used it for 14 years and they recently decided to build a brick version, so the old pavilion was up for sale at offers over £50. Nocton's offer of £51 was successful. So a low loader lorry was hired for the day, at the cost of £300, and the pavilion was transported in one piece across the countryside back to its old home in Nocton where it now sits beside the pavilion erected in 1989 when the club was reformed. This pavilion was actually the former Woodhall Spa Bowls Club pavilion. This arrived "flat-packed" and was erected by the club members in 1980.

Reunited with their old pavilion

Old Pavilion in situ

An article in the local press reported that 'February 2000 brings financial problems to the Nocton Cricket Club. The piece of land that has been used as the Cricket pitch for many years, the ridge and furrow field, between Nocton and Dunston, was part of the Glebe Land that until recently belonged to the Lincoln Diocesan Trust and Board of Finance. This three acres of old pasture was sold to Mr Clarke of Nocton Ltd last year, with a lease attached to it ensuring that the Cricket Pitch remained. But the new landowner

requires the Cricket club to fence the boundary to allow him to keep his sheep on the rest of the field during the summer and winter months. The fence is required to be made of a four foot high galvanised wire mesh and it is 400 metres around the playing area and the quote for this is £2000. The club have been given 18 months to raise the money and install the fence otherwise they are in breach of their lease and will lose their playing facilities'. Yes, the club did raise the money, by kind donations, many fund raising events, and a generous low quotation.

Our final extract from a Parish Magazine is from the July 2005. When Nocton Cricket Club had an enjoyable Village -v- Village Match on Sunday 22nd May 2005 with juniors, regulars, and irregulars forming mixed teams. A draw was declared when there was thunder and lightning at about 7pm, so the cricket had to finish and they were compelled to start the barbeque! It was good to see a group of former cricketers and supporters come to join the present players for tea, although it was too cold for them to stay long!

In July 2006, the Nocton Cricket Club showed their appreciation to David Glew for seventeen years of dedication to the Club, since coming to the village to live, by presenting him with a Silver Cup with the inscription "David Glew - Nocton C.C. - Lifetime Achievement Award - 23.7.2006".

David Glew, beams cutting his cake with the Silver Cup

View from the Cricket Ground towards the Church and Village

CHAPTER 15
Back to the Village along the Bridle Path

From the present Cricket Club car park we will look towards the north and see the church which like cricket has been around for a great number of years. To the left of the church there are many recently built dwellings. The vicarage was built in the early 1950's after the previous one was demolished and another house was built in the garden, this was destroyed by fire in 1996, the present dwelling on the site has been built much more in character and style with the older buildings of this part of the village. The homes now known as "Wray's Yard" are cottages, farm buildings and barns that have been converted into dwellings, in 1998, with two new houses in the crewyard.

The photo, opposite, was taken in 1981, from about the same position, somewhere near the cricket ground, showing Mr and Mrs Smart's new home, Park Farmhouse on the extreme right and the farm buildings in Wrays Yard on the left.

As we return to the village on the old carriage road, we come to a cross roads, which is the Bridle Path from Nocton to Dunston.

Bridle Path showing the Light Railway lines

This photo shows the Light Railway lines, and these rails would have travelled parallel with the Carriage Road. There was a junction that led the railway into the Railhead, while one line went past Top Lodge and then up to the Heath.

"The Heritage Cow"

On a wall as we approach the village, there is a modern sculpture. This is made out of old farm tools and designed by the schoolchildren – the first black and white cow that has lived in Nocton! If we look straight ahead, we see part of the Old Row built in 1841, on your right is Bridle Way Villa where the Noble's used to live. In April 1963, Cyril Noble was described as the oldest native of the Village as he celebrated his 78th Birthday.

Mr and Mrs Cyril Noble

Mr Cyril Noble left school at the age of 14 and for two years was employed at the Vicarage as a footman. He then went on to learn to be both a joiner and wheelwright, a business that was also conducted in the village by both his father, the late Mr Joseph Noble and his grandfather, from the buildings on the right hand side of the path. These buildings were about to be demolished in the 1980's, but were reprieved at the last moment and were reroofed to form two garages.

Demolition of the Wheelwright's Workshop

Inside showing the wheels, beams and pullies

The 1925 Particular of Sale mentions that Mr J. Noble was the tenant of Carpenters Farm, a small holding of 6.578 acres at a rent of £19 3s 0d, while Mr S Noble was a tenant of 4.226 acres at the rent of £9 15s 0d.

Noble's field with cattle and donkey

These fields with some buildings were behind Shooters Lodge. The outbuildings of this house was the Blacksmiths Forge, when the Estate was sold in 1925.

Wheelwrights/blacksmiths on the right in the 1900s

From the 1891 Census, we find that John Atkin was the Blacksmith and that he was living next door to Sylvester Noble described as a Wheelwright. The Dennises moved into Shooter's Lodge, which had been built by Norman Hodgson in 1912, when they first came to Nocton in 1919, before they moved into the Hall. Shooters Lodge was turned into a residential home for the elderly in 1970 and run by Joan and Bill Fenner for nine years. This Photo was taken before the wall was taken down to make Car Parking in front of the Front Door.

Shooters Lodge taken about 2000, before the garden wall was knocked down to make a vehicle access to the Front Door

Across the road is the Post Office, although it has not always been in this building, for we mentioned the Old Post Office at the beginning of Chapter 4. It was a post office when the 1891 Census was carried out for John Pullen, aged 47, lived there and he was described as a Railway Plate Layer. We have come across adverts, in the Church magazines, for R.H.Ash, who described himself as a Grocer, Newsagent, and Tobacconist, operating from the Post Office, Nocton. He was the Post Master from 1944 until about 1951, when Miss.O.Waite took over. She was in charge of the shop and post office for seventeen years. A Postal investigation, in 1968, brought to light the fact that "Nocton" is unique in the postal sense, as there is no other office of the same name anywhere in the world. The nearest was "Noctor" in the famous Blue Grass region of Kentucky in the U.S.A. In 1969, Al Bee took over as the Postmaster. The Estate owned the building and one of the conditions of tenureship was that it had to be open early in the morning so that the estate workers could buy any thing they required for the day such as cigarettes or "baccy".

This account of Al and Barbara Bee's wedding came from The S.P.C.Magazine.

St. Peter's Church at Dunston was the scene of a very pretty wedding on Whit Monday, 1949, when Miss Barbara Dawson, of Dunston, was married to Mr. Albert Bee, of Nocton. Both are well known by all estate workers, as Barbara is a keen Church worker, assistant organist and Sunday School teacher, and Albert being a member of Nocton Cricket Club and a former choir boy of Nocton Church Choir. The bride was given away by her grandfather, Mr. Wilkinson.

She had five bridesmaids in attendance - four grown ups and one small child. A reception was held at Dunston Village Hall and attended by over 240 guests. The presents were numerous and included a wireless set and a pig, also a biscuit barrel from the Choir and Sunday School. A feature of the wedding was the archway formed of cricket bats and wickets by Albert's colleagues of the Cricket Club, who presented him with a barometer. Albert is the son of Mr. and Mrs. Bert Bee, foreman of the Home Section of the Estate.

The future home of the happy couple will be at Nocton, where the bridegroom is employed on the Estate as lorry driver – a situation he has held for the past eleven years, and Barbara works in the Post Office and Village Shop in Dunston.

Al and Barbara Bee's Wedding

1981 – The Post Office looking towards the Village Green

Barbara started working in Dunston Post Office in 1945 helping her Mother. In 1969, when Al became the Postmaster Barbara joined him at Nocton. During that time they had to get up at 5.15 every morning to be ready to sort the mail for deliveries in Potterhanworth, Dunston as well as Nocton. It was in September 1987 that Al and Barbara retired and looked forward to a well earned rest. They were presented with gifts by Jim Smart and Frank Meechan, and a bouquet was presented to Barbara by the oldest resident, Lizzie Jackson.

Their smallest bridesmaid

1987 - Lizzie Jackson presenting Barbara Bee with a bouquet of flowers on her and Al's retirement from the Post Office with Frank Meechan on the left and Mr Smart on the right

Al and Barbara have both been, and still are, keen gardeners. They grew lots of vegetables winning many prizes at the local WI Produce Show, and were always most generous with any surplus that they had. The inside of the Post Office was very different in 1987 to how it looks today.

Inside the Post Office and Village Store

The three local post ladies and Frank Meechan, the postman

The three post ladies were Janet Hewitt for Dunston, Linda Marshall for Nocton, and Joan Paterson for Potterhanworth. Frank Meechan was "Postman Pat", delivering to the businesses and outlying homes and any parcels or packages that were too large for the post ladies to carry on their bikes.

The Butlers took over from the Bees and only stayed for eighteen months. So in March 1989, Shirley and David Emans took over the running of the Post Office and the Village Shop. They introduced an "Off Licence" after getting a Legal Covenant removed which prevented the sale of alcohol, this of course meant that the opening hours were extended to 8 pm. When Roy Bellamy gave up the paper round, they took over the round which involved preparing the daily papers for the paper boys and girls to deliver before they went to school, and the Echo after school. They had an Electric Bread Oven installed which produced lovely fresh bread and buns, and as a special treat, croissants on Sundays. The aroma lingers on, even to this day! In April 1993, there was an attempted armed robbery and Shirley stood her ground and with

brave handling and a few carefully chosen words the uninvited visitor left empty handed. She was awarded the Certificate of Valour by the Post Office for her bravery. The local Doctor's Surgery delivered medicines to the Shop for their patients to collect. When David & Shirley retired in 2003, they did not sell the business as a going concern and the post office was then reduced to part time and the letters are now sorted in Lincoln. Ann Kennedy has taken over the Echo Round with two paper boys helping her out. We were without a daily paper delivery in the village for three years but now there is a daily paper delivery run by the Newsagents from Metheringham. Mrs Glynis Scafton has taken over as the sub postmistress and the post office is only open 19 hours a week on four days, with the collection at 1pm and 5.15 – so you must do some planning if you wish to send anything that needs a receipt. If you take a letter for recorded delivery at 1.30 on a Tuesday, the recipient will not receive it until Friday. We are better off than Potterhanworth, who have lost their Post Office altogether, and any undelivered parcels are returned to the Main Sorting Office in Lincoln for them to collect. And talking about Paper Rounds, in 1960 it was reported that Mrs D Redshaw had delivered newspapers in the district for nearly nineteen years and she never had a day off for sickness. Her earliest start was on a Sunday at 6.30 am. She estimated that she cycled about ten miles each day, for 364 days a year for nearly nineteen years makes a total of 70,000 miles give or take a few.

THE STANDARD, FRIDAY, FEBRUARY 19th, 19

Cycled 70,000 miles

Mrs Doris Redshaw cycled 70,000 miles delivering papers in the locality. She retired in 1960

CHAPTER 16
Old Row and moving towards Embsay House

A glass Slide photo of the Old Row and Main Road

The same view with a Telephone Box and the Water Pump

The Post Office cum Village Store was on the north corner of this terrace of properties. The Old Row now called the Old Ten Row was built in 1841, there were more than 10 dwellings when they were first built, each one had just one room up and one room down, over the years two cottages have been made into one. Now there are just five dwellings in the Row. Ted Redshaw and his wife Freda lived in one, and it was possible to see where the second staircase had been.

Eileen and George Moulds started their married life in the Old Row, and some of Eileen's relations came over from Liverpool to visit and they had their photos taken by the Water Pump.

The Water Pump also acted as the Notice Board for the Cricket Club for they used to pin up the fixture list to the wooden casing.

1954 Eileen's friends Joan Davenport and Monica Francis showing the two water pumps that were there at this time.

The Redshaw family had lived at No 2 Main Road for many years. The house was built of stone in 1875, 18inch thick walls, with no damp course. It had a pantry and dairy and stone steps to the bedrooms. It also had a letterbox near the outside door but not many details are known about the collection of letters. There is a photo of Mrs Mary Ann Redshaw with four of her children taken in the early 1900's, outside the family home.

Mrs Mary Ann Redshaw with four of her children taken in the early 1900's

In the early 1900's, life was very primitive for the estate workers, no mains water, they saved rain water in wooden tubs. The drinking water was collected from the village pump. No inside flush toilets, outside and down the garden path was the vault lavatory, the contents of which would have been put on the gardens. Later on it was a bucket which the council's dilly cart emptied once a week, so on that day all the windows and doors were kept firmly shut until the smell had gone. Man had been to the Moon and back before there was a water toilet at No. 2.

No 2 Main Road – early 1950's

Sheila and Fred at their Wedding Reception – June 1955

Most gardens had fruit trees, Plum, Pear, and Apple, there is still one growing in the garden of No. 2, its called "Peasegoodnonsuch", delicious whether cooked or eaten raw, and an apple could weigh up to 16 ozs.

There were eight boys and four girls in the Redshaw family – nearly all the boys were employed on the Estate. Albert, Fred, and Len served in the World War II – Fred with the Royal Artillery in Egypt, Burma, and India. Albert was a prisoner of war in Italy.

Here is a picture taken for the magazine Land Worker, captioned "Challenge" it shows the Redshaw family, John Henry (father), Herbert, Edward, George, William and Fred.

Their guests – June !955

Photo taken for the Land Worker magazine captioned "Challenge" shows the Redshaw family who all worked on the Smiths Potato Estates, John Henry, the father, Herbert, Edward, George, William and Fred

1955's Photo of No 2 Main Road showing the apple tree

After the War, Fred worked on the Estate as woodman, (we had a photo in the Woodyard in an earlier chapter)

It was in June 1955 that Sheila and Fred were married in Nocton Church and held their wedding reception in the Village Hall. They started married life living at No 2 with Fred's Mother. At this time Fred would drive a Combine during the Harvest and a Lorry the rest of the time. Towards the end of his life, he worked as an agricultural carpenter. Fred and Sheila celebrated their silver wedding anniversary by going on a Mediterranean cruise and Fred died later that year. He was a member of the Royal British Legion and the Ripon Lodge of the Manchester Unity of Oddfellows.

Fred on a Combine

For nearly 30 years he was Verger and sexton at Nocton Church and also a bell ringer.

Fred's father had been the founder secretary of the Nocton Branch of the National Union of Agricultural and Allied Workers. He was succeeded by his son, Bill and in 1956, Fred became secretary of the branch which covered members living in Nocton and Dunston and was one of the largest in the Lincoln District.

Being a branch secretary took a lot of Fred's spare time. It meant collecting monthly Subscriptions.

He would go to the Red Lion at Dunston one Saturday night in the month, with the landlord's permission of course. Funeral and accident claims and other problems would mean a report being sent to the district organiser.

Front Cover of the Land Worker Magazine

A Christmas Card with the caption "You Two Might Be A Thing Of The Past But I'm Not Going To Be"

It was said at his funeral service "His philosophy of life was neither haunted by the past, nor over anxious about the future, but content to find happiness in the joy of the present moment"

The Nocton Branch of the National Union of Agricultural and Allied Workers

Fred and Sheila's Garden about 1980

Sheila has written this piece about the couple who were living in Embsay Cottage, Harry and Lizzie Jackson, in 1955, when she first came to Nocton and she was their neighbour. They bought a new washing machine in April 1959 from the Lincoln Co-operative Society.

"They were a remarkable couple who did many good things for the village right up to their dying day. Harry was very good at writing, in 1970 he started the very first scrapbook for the Nocton Friendship Club. Harry Jackson was born at Sturton by Stow, he worked for many years at Embsay House. He was a gardener and sometimes chauffeur during Mr Ireson's term of office as Estate Manager. He was well known for his Council work, and his association with Nocton Parish Council which lasted over 42 years He was first elected to the Parish council on July 9th 1930 and served for eight years, resigning in April 1938 to become clerk, a post he occupied for a record thirty one years. Following a break of one year after giving up the clerkship, Mr Jackson re-joined the Parish Council in May 1970 for a further three year period. Mr Jackson fought very hard on Nocton's behalf at the North Kesteven Council's Housing Committee to have eight new bungalows for the elderly erected in Nocton rather than in Metheringham. And on his retirement he and his wife moved into No 2 Wellhead Lane.

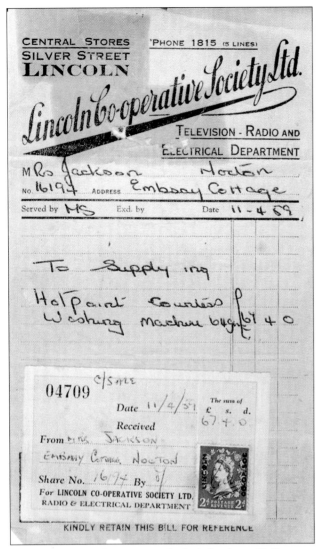

Lincoln Co-operative Society receipt for the Jackson's new Washing Machine

Recent photo of Embsay cottage

Harry and Lizzie Jackson outside no 2 Wellhead Lane

He also served as a school manager from 1934 to 1970, not many people serve such committees for 36 years. He was also on the Village Hall committee for 27 years, from when it first opened and Treasurer for 12 years. He said in 1970, "Nocton is a very quiet village, and it hasn't altered a great deal. Although about 60 new dwellings have been put up in my time here." When he relinquished his position on the Council, he was sent many letters of appreciation from the Nocton Parish Council; Mr J. Freeman, Surveyor and Chief Public Health Inspector, of North Kesteven District Council; G. R. Scott, Director of Education for County of Lincoln-Parts of Kesteven; and J.E.Blow, Solicitor for the same Education Committee; T.L.Hill, the Clerk of the Council, North Kesteven Rural District Council; Mr V.S.Shepherd of the Kesteven Association of Parish Councils; Nocton Village Hall Management Committee; and Miss K.I.Turner, a teacher at Nocton County Primary School.

He sadly died on 13th November 1973, leaving behind Lizzie, who was also a great worker for the village and she was given a presentation from the Friendship Club on 9th May 1988. Here are some of the facts that were gleaned for that occasion. Lizzie had been born on 14th May 1902 at Washingborough Fen, Lincoln, the family moved soon after to the Grange Cottages, Nocton Heath and she attended Nocton School when Alice Tether and Mr David Bratt were the teachers. She left school when she was 13 years old to go into service at Newport in Lincoln. At one time she worked for the 'Bomber' Harris family and for J. Walters the auctioneer of Woodhall Spa when the wages were £6. a year. She married Harry Jackson on 13th March 1926 at Hough on the Hill Church near Grantham. The couple lived in Embsay Cottage, Nocton from March 1926 until November 1972 when they both moved to the new bungalow at 2, Wellhead Lane, Nocton. The information says that she attended The Water Rat Chapel, Dunston Fen regularly until she was confirmed at Blankney Church in 1929.

Her interests included playing cricket for the ladies team in the 1930's and was one of the "tea ladies" who organised and made the delicious salad teas for which the club was renowned until the Cricket Club closed in the late 1970's. (The Cricket Club was reformed

Lizzie Jackson receiving a Certificate in 1988, from Mrs Martindale of Age Concern

in 1989 with friendly matches within the village for the first year) Lizzie was a member of the Mothers' Union for 55 years during which time she twice held the office of Secretary and Treasurer. She was a member of the Parochial Church Council for many years and was appointed Church Warden in 1977. A founder member of the Women's Institute and was appointed the first treasurer and remained a committee member until the WI closed in the early 1980's. (It was reformed in 1989). Lizzie was a founder member of the Nocton Village Hall and she served on the committee for many years and still (in 1988) holds the post of representative of the Church Council on the present Nocton Village Hall Management Committee. When the Friendship Club was formed in 1965, she was a founder member and still regularly attends meetings and club outings. Lizzie was a keen Whist Player for many years and she held whist drives in

her own home for the Church Funds and after the Village Hall was burnt down, she raised funds for the rebuilding of the hall and since 1979 she had raised over £850. And she even found time to help with the Sheep Dog Trials that were held annually since 1973. She would contribute to any charity which has had a fundraising event eg. The baby unit on Nocton Ward at the County Hospital. She has never been known to refuse a request for help and her friends at the Friendship Club all joined together that evening to say a big "Thank-You" to this wonderfully generous lady for her long and outstanding service to the village of Nocton. Lizzie Jackson died on 16th November 1993 aged 91 years.

This also acts as a summary of the activities that were going on in the village from March 1926 to about May 1988. And the next Port of Call is Embsay House.

CHAPTER 17
Mrs Ireson and her Garden Parties

Embsay House bears the date 1867 and is built of stone under a slate roof and is surrounded by a large garden.

Embsay House

As we have said before, Mr and Mrs Ireson came to Nocton in April 1946, Mr Ireson was busy managing the Estate and Mrs Ireson soon became busy organising the villagers. She was a very good organiser and had a way of delegating duties to people where they were unable to say "No". Ian Green recalled the evening, many, many years ago, when he was in the Social Club with a pint in his hand and Mrs Ireson was there requiring some tables to be moved "Ian can you help me with these tables, please" the reply "But I'm having a drink" "You can put the drink down and help me, your drink will still be there when we have finished moving these tables". One of her first achievements was the building of the three Village Halls in Nocton, Dunston and at Wasps Nest. This of course made a great difference to the social life for every one connected with the village and the Estate. Mrs Ireson was also very good at recording events, she would summon a photographer to attend and the resulting photographs were then stuck into her many scrap books made of brown paper and/or wall paper, but unfortunately she stuck the photos and cuttings in with cellotape which has become discoloured over the years. We are fortunate to still have the original scrap book that she made to record the formation of Nocton WI and the many years that followed. When she left the village in 1966 she wrote in the Scrap Book "I should like this book to be given to Mrs Phyl

Redshaw of Nocton for the interest of Nocton WI." Signed L G Ireson 1966. Mrs Phyl Redshaw in turn gave this scrapbook to Eileen Moulds for safe keeping on 1st December 1992. And now some of the contents are going into print. On the front page is the story of Jerusalem and a card "I shall pass through this world but once….." and Mrs Ireson's Membership Card.

"I shall pass through this world but once. Any good thing, therefore, that I can do, or any kindness that I can show to any human being, let me do it now. Let me not defer it or neglect it, for I shall not pass this way again."

A Postcard from page two of Mrs Ireson's Nocton Women's Institute Scrap Book.

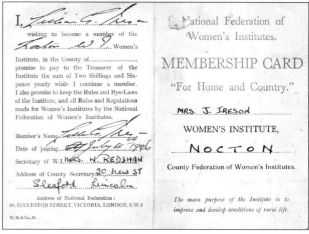

Mrs Ireson's 1946 WI Membership Card

The Nocton WI was formed on 4th July 1946 and for many years an annual Birthday Party was held in the grounds of Embsay House, the First Birthday Party was on 26th June 1947. Nocton WI entertained Metheringham and Potterhanworth Women's Institutes at their first birthday. After competitions and refreshment in the shape of strawberries in the garden of the President, Mrs Ireson, everyone went onto the Village Hall to be entertained by the Drama and Choral Groups, after which supper was enjoyed by all. There will be more about the Nocton WI in the next Volume, about the Handicrafts that were made for Mrs Frank Smith's favourite charity "The Lifeboats" and

First Birthday Party June 26th 1947

the Cups that she gave to encourage Embroidery and Knitting under the guidance of Mrs Ireson.

During the following years more gatherings took place at Embsay House.

1954 has been selected for the interesting Garden Parties that were held in that year.

Saturday 19th June was a brilliantly fine day, it was the Nocton Women's' Institute and Cricket Club Joint Garden Fete. The Fete was opened by Mrs.John Francis, of Boston, who was presented with a bouquet by Cynthia Saunby and Mr Francis received a buttonhole by Robin Hubbard. There was a large company present at the opening ceremony, which was immediately followed English Country and Square Dancing and a Hornpipe given by members of the Women's Institute, with interludes of Fairyland recitations by the children, this entertainment proved very popular and was repeated during the evening.

More Country Dancing

"The Grand Chain"

The Clay Pigeon Shoot took place in the "Noble's Field" opposite Embsay House and competitors came from all parts of the county. The various competitions remained open until about nine o'clock, when a Dance was held in the Village Hall. All the members of the Joint Committee worked hard to make the Fete a success, and through their co-operation and team spirit, they certainly did, because the takings were a record and the Institute and Club each received about £60.

Women's Institute and the Cricket Club Fete June 19th 1954 – Country Dancing

H.M.S. Nocton with l to r Ann Noble with their instructress, Joan Day and Janet Saunby kneeling

Jeane Rasen

Fairyland Figures – Valery Wakefield

Veronica Baker

Sue Picker

Carole Hubbard

Barry Turner

Patrick Hubbard

Later that same month, the Women's Institute celebrated their 8th Birthday with a party in the gardens of Embsay House where they welcomed the Eye Women's Institute from Suffolk and commenced the proceedings with the singing of Jerusalem. The Visitors entertained the members in the evening in the Village Hall.

The 8th Women's Institute Birthday Party- singing Jerusalem with visitors and members outside Embsay House

Eye Women's Institute entertaining Nocton members at the 8th Birthday Party

The President with members on the Birthday evening

Nocton Estates Football Club held their Garden Fete on Saturday 24th July, in the grounds of Embsay House. This was opened by Alderman and Mrs. G Flintham J.P. at 3 pm. This was followed by the Annual Schoolboys' Challenge Football Match - Dunston v Nocton. The Special Attraction this year, straight from the London Exhibitions, is an Exact Replica of the Coronation Coach and Greys which was kindly loaned by Mrs. Frank Smith. Other events at the Fete were Skittling for a Pig, Bowling for Cockerels, All the old favorite Side Shows and some new ones. In the evening there was Dancing in the Village Hall, when the Chairman, Mr J.W.A.Woods, thanked the referee, Mr Walkley, for his services at the football match which was won

by Nocton He also thanked all those who had helped, especially the refreshment ladies.

The Coronation Coach was the Star Attraction. The coach was loaned to Mrs. Ireson by Mrs. Frank Smith of London, and had been on show at garden fetes in London and Edinburgh. A gleaming quarter sized model of the Coronation Coach, complete with eight horses and twelve splendidly dressed grooms was on display. Everything was exact in every detail, even the elaborate paintings on the sides were faithfully reproduced. The model is 24 feet long and is made of plaster. "It is just as it looked on The Day" said one onlooker "If anything, it looks better in the sunshine." For the Nocton Fete Day was fine and warm in contrast to the cold and showers of Coronation Day the previous year.

This fantastic exhibit was given to the Lincoln Library with a message that read
"Royal Coach and Outriders
Quarter Scale Model
Made for Edinburgh Festival at
The Time of Queen Elizabeth II
Coronation
The Gift of
Smith's Potato Estates Ltd., 1962".

And it was packed away in a box and taken to the cellars where it lay undisturbed for more than 30 years, until it was "discovered" in August 1993 when the library was being cleaned out for a refurbishment. Of course, no one knew anything about it, other than it was "The Coronation Coach and Horses". But the Lincolnshire Echo soon came to the rescue, and several people wrote in with the above information and also to say that it had been the centre attraction at a "Coronation Memoirs Exhibition" at the Bailgate Methodist Church where it was seen by a crowd of 500 and helped to raise £22 for the development of the church garden. During 1993 and 1994, the art students of De Montfort University carried out the task of restoring the scale model to its former glory, making a new base as well as casting and moulding some new pieces. It was hoped that it would find a new home on display at The Lawn, but instead it was boxed up into at least two packages, for in 2006, after some intense searching, some of it was found at The Lawn and the rest was found in a different storage area altogether. But thanks go to The Rev Hamish Temple and Mr Roland Christian who have spent quite sometime repairing and painting the Coach and Outriders. They are now in splendid condition and were on display at a Flower Festival at the United Church St Martin's Square, Lincoln in April 2007. Let us hope that a fitting home is found for this unique piece of history.

Quarter scale model of the Royal Coach and outriders. First on display 24th July 1954. Photographed here at the United Church, Lincoln - April 2007

CHAPTER 18
The Men and Women who served the Country in the Second World War

There is no plaque in Nocton to commemorate the men who died from this parish in the Second World War, nor any record of those men and women from our parish who served in the Armed Forces. So we would like to acknowledge their sacrifice here within our book

Much research has been undertaken to try to establish who left Nocton and who did not return. The Commonwealth War Graves Commission has provided a report on casualties with "Nocton" in their next-of-kin details. Private Joseph Alfred Topham, Singalman Bernard Simpson Plumtree, Private Charles Ashton, and Private Eric James Pinner are the listed casualties and further details are along side.

Nocton was fortunate in that most of the serving personnel did return home safely, but some were wounded. Below is a list of people that left and returned, and if a member of your family is not mentioned please get in touch so that they can be added to our records.

Major R.G.F.Howard
Doris Battersby – Wrens
John Bee
Cyril Bee
Arthur Chambers - Wounded in 1944
Dorothy Chambers
Phylls Chambers
Bruce Cummins
Iris Gash - N.A.F.F.I
Harold Harrod
Wilfred Hubbard
Edwin Ingall - Wounded in 1944
Peter Ingall
Tony Jackson
William Melton
George Merryweather – POW for 5 years
L.A.C.Arthur Pask
C.S.M.I.CyrilPask
Sergt. Donald Pask
A.C.2 Ernest Pask
Pte. Roland Pask
Hilda Pygott
Albert Redshaw
Fred Redshaw

Casualties with "NOCTON" in their next-of-kin details, WW 2 Commonwealth War Dead 1939-45

TOPHAM, Private, JOSEPH ALFRED, 4802704, 2nd Bn., Lincolnshire Regiment. 30 May 1940 - 2 June 1940. Age 20. Son of John Robert and Annie Elizabeth Topham, of Nocton, Lincolnshire. Column 45.
DUNKIRK MEMORIAL, France

PLUMTREE, Signalman, BERNARD SIMPSON, 4806008, 101 Sub-Area Beach Sig. Sec., Royal Corps of Signals. 6 June 1944. Age 27. Son of Annie Elizabeth Cummins, of Nocton, Lincolnshire. Grave Ref. 1. C. 18.
HERMANVILLE WAR CEMETERY, France

ASHTON, Private, CHARLES, 4801203, 4th Bn., Lincolnshire Regiment. 26 June 1944. Age 32. Son of Charles and Sophia Ashton, of Nocton, Lincolnshire. Grave Ref. II. F. 8.
TILLY-SUR-SEULLES WAR CEMETERY France

PINNER, Private, ERIC JAMES, 5776240, 6th Bn., Royal Norfolk Regiment. 13 January 1943. Age 24. Son of John and Kate Pinner; husband of Avril May Pinner, of Nocton, Lincolnshire. Grave Ref. 12. E. 10.
CHUNGKAI WAR CEMETERY, Thailand

Also:-
Leonard Redshaw
Margarie Smith WAAF Dambuster Squadron
Jack Smith RAF
Sidney Smith RAF
Ivy Stiff
Christine Towle
Donald Turner
Ben White - Lost an arm as a result of serious wounds in 1944
Johnny Young

Driver E W Jackson

October 1943 – Mr and Mrs W Jackson, of Ellerby Cottage, Nocton Heath, were notified by the War Office that their second son, Driver E W Jackson was reported missing in June 1942, is now presumed to have been killed in action in Tobruk.

The letter stated that Driver Jackson was sent with his vehicle to a minefield to collect some mines which had been detonated but not laid. Shortly after he had reached the minefield an explosion was heard from that direction.

Twenty five years of age Driver Jackson had been a driver for the Lincs Road Car for three years when he was called up in 1940. He became a driver in the R.A.S.C., and went to the Middle East in 1941. Mr and Mrs Jackson had two other sons, the elder one serving in the R.A.F., and the youngest in the Lincolnshire Regiment.

Driver Jackson's name was not included on any Village 'Role of Honour'. Forty five years later, it was added to the 'Role of Honour' in Harmston Parish Church. Mr Edward Hennell had persevered for many years, his father had employed Driver Jackson's father at the time war broke out.

March 1943 - Ivy Stiff was a member of the "B Crew" at Fairwood Common, Swansea

Ivy and her friend at Rhyll in July 1945

While the parishioners, listed on previous page, served away from the village, many of the remaining men joined the Home Guard and continued their daily working life, but being on alert and ready for any eventuality that might crop up. Wray's Yard was the meeting place. There are two photographs of the Home Guard, one showing mostly Nocton recruits and the other has a much larger catchment area – Metheringham, Dunston and Potterhanworth names are listed.

The Nocton list is A Bee, P Ward, J Wass, W. Elkington, G.Kidder, Bill Pygott, T.Glossop, G.Saunby, Peter Roberson, Bill Jackson, Tony Jackson, Ted Scoffins, G. Redshaw, E.Redshaw, H.Gash, Marshall Salter, J.Day, G Hawood and Harry Carratt.

Mostly Nocton men in the Home Guard

The Ministry of War had commandeered Nocton Hall as a convalescent home and many of the local ladies worked there as orderlies and nursing staff. At the Manor House, Mrs Kennington's spirited patriotism in May 1942 resulted in "The County's First Outworking Experiment", using the untapped part-time labour of older women, girls and youths to sort and test nuts and bolts for a Lincoln factory. The idea was that some routine work could be brought out to the villages where there was some part-time labour available. The first assignment was testing and inspecting 35,000

Mrs Kennington's War Effort at the Manor House: (left to right) Mrs G Kennington, Mrs Daisy Brown, Mrs Kath Young, Mrs Chris White, Marion Carlton, Mrs A Tye neé Glossop at the back and Mike the dog

The Home Guard in Wray's Yard

nuts followed by making 10,000 joints and packing them for a Lincoln firm. About 30 women, girls and youths took part in this project including Aggie Glossop who is now Mrs Tye, she was a star turn at the benches.

It wasn't until 1948 that the Estates Company sold the Hall and 200 acres to the Air Ministry and by 1951 it was a General Military Hospital. After much money was spent to upgrade the Maternity Wing and the Operating Theatres, it was closed in 1985. Another story.

Thomas Overton M.M. 1920 – 2006

Tom was living at Boston, Lincolnshire, when he joined the army in the 1939-45 war. After the war he came to live in the Bardney and Nocton area as an agricultural worker. He worked for three different employers on the same estate, Dennises, Smiths Potato Estates and Nocton Farms for over 50 years. He was awarded the Military Medal in 1943.

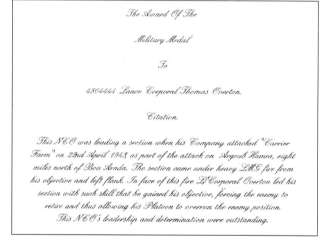

Tom Overton's Citation

List of members

CHAPTER 19
A Summary for the next Volume

Village Hall

Leaving Embsay House, we retrace footsteps to the Post Office and turning left soon come to the much mentioned Village Hall. This was the Social Centre for the Village after 1947.

Village Hall in 1947

There were regular Whist Drives, Dances and Bingo evenings. In the mid 1960's there was a Tufty Club. It was on a fateful night in January 1979 that the Village Hall was burnt down. Trevor and Pat Green were involved with Social Club at the time and she said "The trouble is the hall is priceless to the villagers for all of the clubs meet here, and now the social life will be dead in Nocton". The site had to be cleared and the wooden hall was replaced by a brick building. As is often the case, the building was underinsured. The whole village rallied around to help make some money, whist drives were held in Potterhanworth and Dunston and clubs had to go to other meeting places for nearly two years. David Rumbelow came up with idea of holding a Sheep Dog Trial which was held on July 21st, with special buses from Dunston, Metheringham and Nocton, and this event was repeated for many years to raise money for the Village Hall.

So within two years, The New Hall was opened on 1st November 1980. And the members of the Social Club gathered together to allow Don Turner to draw the first pint, for he was the retiring Secretary of the N.V.H.Social Club.

The organisers of the Youth Club during the 1980's were Philip and Joan Franklin. The Friendship Club started by Mrs Smart in 1966 was a thriving organisation until most of the members moved to Metheringham and latterly were without transport, the club unfortunately closed a few years ago. Bingo was held on Sunday evenings, for many years. The Social Club now uses part of the Village Hall and the main

Retiring secretary of the Nocton Village Hall Social Club, Mr Don Turner, pulling the first pint at the official opening last Saturday. The new village hall is to be officially opened on November 1.

New Village Hall reopens in November 1980

Friendship Club Christmas Party 1993

function room is let out to the WI for their monthly meeting, the Art Group hold weekly meetings during school times, the Heritage Trail Association use the hall for making up their projects, and to any member of the village who wishes to book it for a function, such as a children's birthday party, wedding receptions, funeral wakes or just to meet some friends.

Tom Foods sold the Estate in 1975 having arranged a tenancy agreement with the Nocton Parish Council for the Recreation Field, this was 3.795 acres and situated behind the Village Hall. The Tenancy was for 30 years from 25th March 1973 at the rent of £4 per annum. In 2003, the present Landowner did not wish to renew the lease for this field.

Halls Yard

Returning to the Village Green, on our left we pass Hall's Yard, which had been a working Farm, but since the 1960's it was mainly used for storage until it was sold in the late 1980s and now there is a House in the Crew yard, the Barn is a home, the Out buildings converted into a single storied dwelling and other barns into another house.

Hall's Yard 1983

Park Farm Yard/Wray's Yard

On the opposite side of the road is a well designed group of buildings that have been converted into homes from the Edwardian Model Farm which was built in 1913, as one of the last projects that Norman Hodgson oversaw, because the family left the village on 26th July 1919. The large Barn, that had the Light Railway running through the middle of it, is now a large house, the Stock buildings have been made into charming semi-detached homes, in the crewyard are two new stone houses and completing the complex, the three cottages have been turned into one home.

Mrs Castle in Park Farm Cottages

The 1891 Census gives most of the properties numbers, some make sense, some do not and so assumptions are made. William Roberts was a Farmer who was born in Ragnall in Nottinghamshire and he lived in the centre of village – was it at Park Farm? As mentioned earlier he also played cricket for the Nocton team.

Information gleaned from The Particulars of Sale of Nocton Estate in 1925 show that Mr W Wray was in occupation of Park Farm which comprised of 333a. 1r. 37p., paying an annual rent of £416 19s. 10d. It was described as "A Sound Mixed Holding" including a Stone-built Farm House standing in the Village, including three Reception rooms, four Bedrooms, and a Box Room. Outbuildings and a Good Garden. The Ample Homestead included Eight-bay Cart Shed, three covered Crewyards, Boiling House, Stable for eight, Houses for Saddles, Corn, Chaff, Cowes, and Cake, A Barn, and Granary. Also Three Capital Cottages.

William, eldest son of Mr Timothy Wray of Dunston, married Susan, second daughter of Mr Thomas Halkes of Dunston, on 9th June 1897 in their parish church with a quiet wedding owing to the ill health of Mrs Halkes. It is not known the exact date that William, Susan and some of their five children came to live at Park Farm, for they are not recorded in the 1901 Census. But in the April 1904 Nocton Church Magazine it states that Mr William Wray had been elected to serve on the Branston District Council as representing Nocton's interests. He was also elected to the Parish Council and was a Nocton Parish Constable along with H.Brown, F.Tye, and T.Chapman. and he was a School Manager at this time as well.

William Wray in Park Farm Stackyard

William and Susan's eldest son, Leslie was killed in the First World War in the Battle of Cambrai on the 20th November 1917, aged 19 years. The family had a Stained Glass Window placed in the Church in his memory.

Susan Wray

Leslie Halkes Wray killed in action 30th November 1917

When William Wray had his dispersal sale sometime after 1925, he handed down the memory that the times were bad, for he was bid only half a crown for two good Garden Seats and nobody bought them, so after the sale he bought them himself.

Later Wray's Yard was used by the Dennises and then Smiths Potato Estates for their Horses and then later for the Cattle, and the sheep did come into the yard for there was a sheep dip in one of the corners. Some of the machinery was also stored in this Yard.

Wray's Yard in the 1950's – Maintenance

The Manor House

It is believed that this house was built between 1805 and 1810.

By 1925, the Manor House was described as, a fine old stone-built House with walled garden, let to Mr.W.E.Pepper on a six month tenancy at an annual rent of £26.10s.0d.

The family had been in the village for a number of years. Mr Pepper was a School Manager in 1904 and in April 1908 he presided over a parish meeting to discuss the matter of the monies in the Clothing Club.

This family also lost a member in the First World War, their daughter, Dorothy who was a nurse, died not in action but from a infected wound she received from opening a tin of meat.

The Dennis family moved into the Manor House, in 1927 and remained there until the Estate was sold in 1939. Mrs Kennington came to live at the Manor, and her spirited patriotism in May 1942 resulted in "The County's First Outworking Experiment" which was mentioned in the previous chapter.

For many years the House was divided into three homes but now it back to being one residence.

The Manor House taken in 1942

Car leaving the Pheasantry, the Manor House is out of the picture on the left (Reproduced by kind permission of the Ray Hooley collection)

The Village Green

This area has always been the centre of the village although it may not have been the centre of activities, everyone had to pass this way to the School and the Church.

In 1978, Nocton won the Best Kept Village Competition and Mr Jim Smart planted a Cherry Tree to commemorate the event. This has now grown into a large tree.

The Best Kept Village in 1978

The Green in the Spring of 1991

Banqueting Hall/Co-operative Stores/Pheasantry

The track leads off to the left from the Village Green to this building. From this side it looks like any normal stone building, but on the East Front it is decorated to look like a Grand House, but most of the windows are painted on - even one is left slightly open, and would have looked straight across the lawns to the Hall. It is said that it was used by the Hobarts to entertain their sporting friends after a Day's Shooting. At one time it was reputed to be a Lodging House, where any traveller could turn up for a meal and they would be sat down to the table with a plate of food put in front of them.

In the 1872 White's Directory the Co-operative Stores is mentioned and states that Luke Teather was the Manager and he was also the parish clerk. Luke was still there for the 1901 census which says that at the Co-operative Stores Luke Tether, the Grocer, lived with his wife Sarah who was a Sewing Mistress at the School and their daughter Alice who was an Infant Teacher. For many years it was used as two

cottages for estate workers, but was allowed to get into disrepair and was sold to a private buyer about 1990. It is now called the Pheasantry.

The School

There has been a school in the Village for many years, for Alderman Glasier, he was born in 1807, recalled trudging in all weather down the Coachman's Drive from the Glebe Farm, on the Heath. He attended Miss Brackenbury's school against the church (not the present church)

Children playing outside of School

The Marquis of Ripon was responsible for the building of the present School in 1869, and he supported the school as did the Hodgson Family. In 1912, Norman Hodgson set up a 30 year lease with Kesteven County Council for the School and House in 1.54 acres of ground and the rent of £40 per annum. Mr David Bratt was the Headmaster for 40 years.

Mr David Bratt who was headmaster for 40 years

He was the enumerator for the 1891 Census, which states that he was 50 years old and had been born in Chester while his wife Eliza was four years younger and had come from Walsall in Staffordshire and three of their children had been born in Nocton. Mrs Bratt died in July 1899 from burns – she had been cooking on her own in the kitchen when her apron and clothing caught fire with fatal consequences. There are many reports in the Church Magazines about evening classes being conducted in the school room, anything from Laundry work to Book keeping.

Mr Emmison also liked teaching the children of Nocton for he stayed 38 years and 10 months.

Mr Emmison with his pupils

The Vicarage

The Vicarage with Church in the Background

Vicarage taken at the turn of the century

Mr Henry Footman was in Residence when the 1891 Census was carried out. He was living in the Vicarage with his wife Catherine and their daughter, Catherine a niece and a visitor called Catherine Payne. They had two servants as well as a cook who had been born in Deeping St Nicholas, while the Housekeeper came from Holbeach.

The Rev Footman was vicar of Nocton for 21 years The village revolved around the Church activities as the Church Magazine religiously describes and there will be more on living in Nocton during 1898 and 1899 in the next volume. The Footmans organised the Garden Parties for the Church and they helped with the formation of the Young Men's Club by converting some of their outbuildings into a Reading Room and a room with a Billiard Table.

The Young Men's Club Building taken in 1980 now converted into Nutwood

Canon Footman was well liked among the villagers although he had been at loggerheads with John Hodgson, but on their deathbeds in 1902 they exchanged notes of goodwill. Maurice Footman along with Kate Norgate wrote "Some Notes on the History of Nocton", a work of great dedication and an invaluable historic work. He also took many Lantern Slides of Nocton that show the way of life in the 1890's.

Canon Footman

Canon Chard

Canon Chard came to Nocton in 1911 and stayed for 32 years.

Enoch Brown – Gardener at the Vicarage

Mr Richard Semper

Delivering milk to the Vicarage

The large Garden required many gardeners to keep it in the beautiful state that it appears on the photographs that were taken, we have a photo of Enoch Brown taken in the Vicarage Garden. He was also on many of the Committees in the Village as well as being a Parish Councillor. The Rev Chard liked to help with the Haymaking as this photograph shows

Rev. Chard Gathering Hay

And finally A view of The Church taken in 1970.

The Vicarage was a huge building with 63 doors all painted white. These were washed every spring and every autumn. The Building was pulled down in the 1950s, and a new one built on the flower beds.

There will be more on the Church and a whole chapter or two on R.A.F. Nocton Hall in the next volume.

Church taken in 1970.

CHAPTER 20
Conclusion – The decline of an Estate Village?

We started off asking the question is Nocton an Estate Village? And came to the conclusion that an Estate village was "A Village wholly or largely built by a single gentry or aristocratic landowner in a place where he had his principle residence. Generally the housing would be architect designed and of a superior quality and the village might have a school and/or village hall to match." During your tour of the Parish of Nocton you will have seen that everything rotated around the Hall and the workers on the Estate, until the two were separated in the time of the Dennises. But the owners of the Estate have, until recently, employed and housed the residents of Nocton and looked after their welfare. It was during the 1960's that the odd plot of land was sold off and this gradually increased during the 1980's bringing in new residents that did not work for the Estate. As the Estate became more mechanised less men were required to do the work, gradually some left to become engineers for British Telecom or to work for Rustons or any other occupation. These men with their families moved away from the village either to Lincoln or to one of the surrounding villages.

This piece written about Frank Smith in the 1970's was true then but it has been slowly declining ever since "The Estate, today, is a very valuable asset to the Company, (then a bit about the history since Saxon times) and the concluding paragraph says – Nocton, it is very evident, has seen more changes than many an English village so deep in the heart of the country. Formerly bound up in the fortunes of the Hall, Nocton now witnesses large scale commercial farming. It is part of a progressive era in agricultural history, though to see its cottages, a gracious farm or two, a tiny post office cum shop, the quiet stone walls and colourful cottage gardens, one might imagine it to be old-world, peaceful and untouched by the modern spirit of change".

But Nocton is touched by the modern spirit of change. Some of the lorries that come through the village are so long that they have difficulties negotiating all the bends. No, we do not want to go back to the horse with it's cart or carriage, what would we do with all the horse droppings?

The main thing that has changed for Nocton is the Social side. The Social Club is still operating and there are a few clubs – the cricket club, the WI and the Art Group that are well attended.

During the 1890's until about 1950, Nocton had its own Vicar living in the Vicarage. After that, Dunston, Potterhanworth and Nocton were grouped together with the Vicar living in Nocton. Now one Clergyman lives in Branston and looks after that parish, Potterhanworth and Nocton with one service a fortnight held in Nocton Church.

"The Progress" that has happened during the past 50 years has been enormous – what will the next 50 years bring?

Field of Lincolnshire Longwool ewes and lambs – Now a rare sight with the Breed declared a "Rare Breed".

ACKNOWLEDGEMENTS

Acknowledgements for the loan of photographs and information that have been scanned on to the computer.

Ann Barney - Great grand daughter of Herbert Dennis, for the Photographs of the Dennis Family in Chapter 3.
Chris Howard - for all the photographs for Chapter 5
Phyll Sands - for all the Edenbrow photographs in Chapter 13
Joan Barratt
Albert Bee
Bill Chambers
Shirley Emmans
David Glew
Elsie Horton
Tony Jackson
David Ireson
Ann Kennedy
Jean Meechan
Eileen Moulds
Ernest Pask
Mike Rossington
David and Gill Rumbelow
Angela Suttle
Aggie Tye
Edith Wakefield
Margaret Wilford
John Wray
The Staff at Lincoln Central Library for their help with finding the War Graves address.
Also to Carol Bennett for the use of the Parish Magazines before they are deposited at the Lincoln Archives
Trevor Morris for proof reading

These books have been used for reference
Some Notes for a History of Nocton by Kate Norgate and Maurice Henry Footman.
The Lincolnshire Potato Railways by Stewart E Squires.
The Revelations of an Imp by Douglas Craven-Hodgson
A Lincolnshire Lad Looks Back by Len Woodhead.
The Definition of an Estate Village by Dennis Mills
Lincolnshire Almshouses by Linda Crust

And Local Publications
Lincolnshire Life, Lincolnshire Echo,
Lincolnshire Chronicle and the Sleaford Standard.

APPENDIX

CHAPTER 2
1925 Particular of Sale

The Estate as a whole is let to W. Dennis & Sons, Ltd., who let certain portions of the Property in accordance with the following

SCHEDULE OF THE ESTATE AS OCCUPIED

HOLDING.	TENANT.	TENANCY.	AREA. ACRES.	RENT.
HOLDINGS LET. Park Farm, Nocton	Mr. W. Wray	Yearly, 6th April	333·486	£ s. d. 416 19 10
Nocton Rise Farm	Mr. C. E. Howard	Do.	350·665	438 2 6
Wood Farm, Dunston	Mrs. Brown	Life tenant	34·971	33 10 0
Small Holding, Nocton	Mr. S. E. Pask	Yearly, 6th April	29·849	55 15 6
Post Office Farm, do.	Mrs. Dowman	Do.	38·690	61 14 5
School and House, do.	Kesteven C.C.	Lease for 30 years from 1912	1·540	40 0 0
Carpenter's Farm, do.	Mr. J. Noble	Yearly, 6th April	6·464	19 3 0
Small Holding, do.	Mr. S. Noble	Do.	4·226	9 15 0
Manor House, do.	Mr. W. E. Pepper	Six months	·707	26 10 0
Allotments, do.	Various	Do	13·754	21 8 0
Brook House, Dunston	Capt. Hammond	Do.	1·013	45 10 0
White House Farm, do.	Mr. R. Wray	Yearly, 6th April	6·578	39 19 0
Red Lion Inn, do.	Mrs. Scott	Do.	·932	27 10 0
Paddock Farm, do.	Mr. W. Willows	Do.	15·046	39 16 6
Small Holding at do.	Mr. A. V. Hussey	Do.	22·084	48 6 0
Do. do.	Mr. C. Richardson	Do.	57·199	90 19 0
Shoemaker's Farm, do.	Mr. G. Robinson	Do.	12·676	31 7 6
Grotto Lane Farm, do.	Mr. W. Brown	Do.	11·717	31 4 0
The Laurels, do.	Mr. J. Rowston	Do.	·222	13 0 0
Small Holding, do.	Mr. G. Spencer	Do.	5·497	6 16 0
Builder's Yard, Cottage, etc., Dunston	Messrs. Halkes Bros.	Do.	4·052	25 0 0
Yew Cottage, Dunston	Mr. A. Hickson	Do.	·953	6 14 0
Paddock, do.	Mr. W. Semper	Do.	·790	1 4 0
Allotments, do.	Various	Do.	22·525	38 12 0
Cottage, nr. Nocton Wood	Mr. A. Brown	Six months	} ·572	6 5 10
Do. do.	Exors. Baldock	Do.		5 0 6
15 Cottages, Nocton	Various	Do.	—	77 12 9
17 Cottages, Dunston	Do.	Do.	—	112 3 4
			A. 976·208	£1,769 10 8

The Remainder of the Estate is in the occupation of W. Dennis & Sons, Ltd.

LANDLORD'S OUTGOINGS :—

	£ s. d.
Drainage Rates	1,087 19 10
Land Tax	81 1 1
Fee Farm Rent	2 4 10
	£1,171 5 9

The Landlords pay rates on certain Cottages.

CHAPTER 3
The Scoley Family
1898 - Notes from the Parish Registers

Between the 17th of March 1734, when John and Mary Scoley were christened in our church, and the 5th February 1862, when Rebecca Scoley aged 79 was laid to rest in our churchyard, the name of Scoley – sometimes spelt Scholey and sometimes Scoly – occurs no less than 73 times in the Potterhanworth registers. Between the 10th of July, 1775, when Mary, daughter of John and Dorothy Scoley, was baptized, and the 11th of April, 1883, when Justina Scoley aged 88 was buried, the name Scoley – sometimes spelt Scholey – occurs 31 times in the Nocton registers.

From 1737 to 1776 one Scoley or another paid tithe every year to the Vicar of Nocton, the amounts varying from two shillings in 1737 to £5.9s. in 1776, in which year the tithes were commuted.

In modern times, from 1865 to 1873 there was always a Scoley churchwarden of Nocton.

The Rev S. B. Bridges wrote in the Nocton and Potterhanworth Parish Magazine in October 1901 – An Old Friend.

Mrs Emma Scoley, whose burial we record this month, was a daughter of Thomas and Rebecca Scoley of Whitehall Farm, Potterhanworth. She was baptised in Potterhanworth on the 3rd September, 1820, and she was married in the same church on the 23rd of September, 1846, to her cousin, Robert, son of Edward and Justina Scoley of Nocton. For many years Mr. and Mrs. Robert Scoley occupied the Manor Farm at Nocton. After her husband's death in 1875, Mrs Scoley lived at the "Almshouse", and was a regular attendant of the Working Party. Though she left Nocton ten years ago, her memory is still fresh in the minds of all who knew her. She died on Wednesday, the 4th of September, at the home of her daughter, Mrs Bell of Newark, aged 81 years.

CHAPTER 8
GN&GE Agreement

Extract from the Sale Particulars for the Sale of Nocton Hall Estate on 28th day of July, 1925 at 2.30 o'clock.

Under Special Stipulations, it states that the Vendors, W. Dennis & Sons Ltd, shall have every facility for harvesting and storing the 1925 harvest including the exclusive use of the Light Railway and Rolling Stock. The stipulations go on to say that all fixtures belonging to the vendors, such as Potato Boiling Plants, fixed Grinding and Grist Mills, Avery Pig-weighing Machine and cage, and all fixed Pig Huts, together with the Light Railway as laid and the Engines, Trucks, Vans and Sheets used in connection of the purchase be on the Estate and the Warehouses now standing near Nocton Railway Station, including the Electric Lighting Installation therein together with the Telephone Installation serving the Estate, are not included in the Sale, but have been estimated as of the value of £16,000 and shall be taken over by the Purchaser in addition to his purchase money. Also in the stipulations are details of a complicated Agreement between W.Dennis and Sons, Ltd., and the Great Northern and Great Eastern Joint Committee, dated 31st December 1920, under which the Committee at their own cost have constructed Sidings at or near Nocton Station and W Dennis and Sons, Ltd., have repaid to the Committee the cost thereof, in a consideration for which the Committee agreed to allow W.Dennis & Sons, Ltd., a credit of 10% on the amount received by the Committee in every year ending 31st December for the carriage of traffic on the Committee's railway passing to and from the property hereby contracted to be sold during a period of 14 years from the completion of the said Sidings, subject to a proviso that if and whenever the total amount of the credit so allowed should amount to a sum equal to the cost incurred by the Committee in executing the said works the said credit should cease to be allowed. The Purchaser shall be required, subject if necessary to the Committee consenting, to take over the benefit and obligations of this Agreement and shall pay to W.Dennis & Sons, Ltd., upon completion and in addition to his purchase money the sum of £1,438 11s. 6d., being the amount standing as a debit in their books on the 31st December, 1924, in respect of the construction of the said siding.